VECTORWORKS FOR THEATRE

by Steve Macluskie

etpress

Entertainment Technology Press

Vectorworks for Theatre

© Steve Macluskie

First published May 2015
Entertainment Technology Press Ltd
The Studio, High Green, Great Shelford, Cambridge CB22 5EG
Internet: www.etnow.com

ISBN 978 1 904031 82 6

A title within the
Entertainment Technology Press Application & Techniques Series
Series editor: John Offord

CONTENTS

INTRODUCTION

The chapters of this book have been rewritten and adapted from the classroom tutorials and hand-outs I have compiled over the years for the students of the BA Production Technology & Management Programme at the Royal Conservatoire of Scotland.

Chapter 1 investigates the Basic Tool Palette and the main workspace and is intended to be an introduction and reference guide which will be returned to as needed. The following chapters have all been written in response to requests from groups or individuals for practical step-by-step guides to specific tasks.

I have used screengrabs and graphic illustrations as much as possible for clarity and those screengrabs have come from a mixture of Vectorworks 2013, 2014 and 2015 on both Mac and PC.

A basic understanding of how to use a computer is assumed and shortcuts and keystrokes are written for both Mac and PC wherever possible.

Vectorworks is a very easy programme to just open and start drawing, so that's what we'll do.

Enjoy!

1 THE BASIC TOOL PALETTE

Introduction to the Workspace

When you run Vectorworks it will launch into a screen very similar to this.

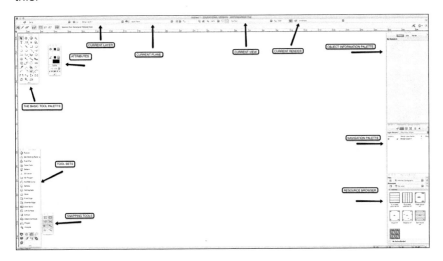

The Main Functions of The Basic Tool Palette

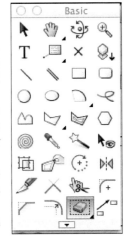

The Basic Tool Palette is your default set of tools. You will come back to this palette time and time again while you are working as it contains the most common tools.

It must be noted that as you select each of these tools a subset of tools and/or preferences becomes available in the top toolbar allowing you further options over the tool you have chosen.

For example, in the screenshot (right) the circle tool is selected. Note that there are multiple options of how I wish to draw my circle.

This format of selecting the tool, then selecting a

tool mode is commonplace throughout the tools of the Basic Palette. Be sure to check and actively select the correct mode for what you are trying to achieve.

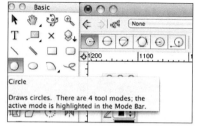

I will start with the Line tool and then go back through the tools from top left to bottom right. Please read the following line tool section thoroughly and then feel free to dip into each tool as necessary. Some will be useful and some not so useful to begin with. Some of the tools are rarely used and some extremely common in theatre CAD work. Don't worry about trying to understand them all just now; things will become clearer as you begin to use the tools properly in your projects.

The Line Tool

Select the line tool and the "Unconstrained / Vertex " Mode (This should be selected by default)

Move your cursor over the main space in the centre of your screen area which is the workspace. Click once to "pin" one end of the line then move cursor away from this first point. Notice how the line stretches from the first "pinned" point. Click again a short distance away and you will have a line drawn on your sheet of virtual paper in the workspace.

This line is still "active" or "selected" since it has a glowing orange appearance.

If you were to click again and draw another line then the new line would become active and this original line would return to a normal looking black line. Make sure you are able to identify which object is "active" before proceeding.

Make sure you have a line selected, as in the screengrab, then let's look at a new area of the screen to the upper right called the "Object Information Palette".

The object information palette will show you the information related to the selected object. This can be quite simple, such as our single line, or very complex with multiple pages of information.

Make sure the "shape" tab is selected as in the screengrab.

This tab will be the most common tab you will use as it displays (and

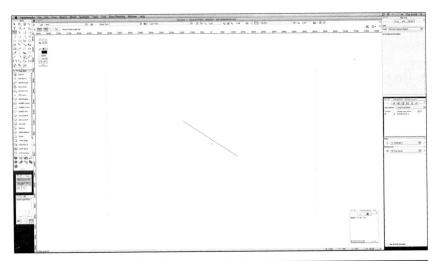

allows you to manipulate) almost all elements of the selected shape.

The line has a "class" of "none" which just means it doesn't belong to any class yet. We can create classes easily such as "act1", "act 2" or "chairs", "tables", etc. and assign objects to them but we'll go into that in another chapter. Just be aware that when you select an object you can see (and change) its class here.

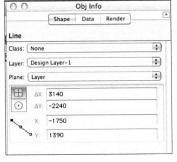

The line is drawn on "Layer" "Design Layer-1". This is a default layer which all objects will be drawn upon until you set up your own layers. Think of layers as physical slices of a 3D space. If I had a 3D model of a theatre it could have layers such as "stage level" "flyfloor" "grid" and also "orchestra pit". These all had physical values or positions above or below a nominated zero or datum layer. The flyfloor layer being 7.5 metres "above" the stage layer and the grid layer being 15 metres above the stage layer. By using layers intelligently when we draw we can make sure that we separate out information which will make our drawing easier to understand and work with. Very simply, Classes are 'what' an object is, Layers are 'where' an object is.

In this example the Plane- Layer information could be thought of as the floor of a building, the workshop floor or the sheet of paper on which we are drawing. It is possible to set up "a working plane" at any orientation within the drawing (and save it) so that you can draw accurately on sloping faces such as rakes. More on this in chapter 3. There is a dropdown option to change to "Screen" which allows you to draw in the same plane as your computer screen no matter what the orientation of the plane. For example, even in an isometric view, a square would be drawn as if stuck to the back of the monitor screen. If this is confusing, don't worry, it will be covered later on; stick to Layer Plane as the default for now.

You will be using the next numerical boxes very shortly.

The DeltaX and DeltaY numbers refer to the distance of the line along the X axis (left to right) and Y axis (bottom to top).

Our line above has travelled 3140 along the X axis and 2240 down the Y axis.

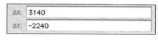

Note that neither of these numbers tell us the length of the line

The X and Y numbers tell us the position of the start position of the line.

Note the numbers around the edge of your working area which should confirm this.

And note this little icon which shows you which point the X&Y numbers above are referring to.

Click the middle and end squares of this graphic; note the X&Y values change but the DeltaX & DeltaY do not. (the delta values may change from positive to negative since the line will be assumed to be travelling in the opposite direction).

All this information is great but what we normally need is the simple length and angle of the line.

At the moment the "absolute" data icon is selected, it looks like a little grid. Click the icon below it, which looks like a circle, and see how the data changes.

This time we have a much more useful L parameter which is "length".

We also have an angle of -35.5 degrees and the XY position of the highlighted box within the drawing area.

I tend to keep this "relative" data option activated for the majority of the work I do.

Manipulating the drawing

All the data we have just looked at is editable by typing directly into the boxes.

Therefore, within the "relative" data screen (as in the screengrab above), click your cursor into the L (length) box and type a new value. When you hit "return" or "enter" on the keyboard the line should ping to the new length. Notice how the "pinned" part of the line is defined by this icon.

For example, if I changed the L Length to 4000 the line will extend down and right to four metres keeping the original point intact. If I click the middle box and change the L length to 5000 the line will extend out both ends keeping the middle "pinned".

If I change the angle (A) to 90° the icon rotates to mimic the orientation of the line on the page.

As well as the very useful Object Information palette we can manipulate all the properties of our simple line by using the mouse and the select tool.

This time, click on the drawn line on the page to select it.

In this screengrab (right) the "Single Object Interactive Scaling Mode" (middle button) is selected which means that our line, when selected in the drawing area, should have blue dots "nodes" at each end like this (below).

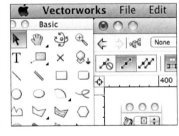

When you move your select cursor on to either of these handles you will be able to click and move either end of the line, therefore manipulating the drawn line by using the mouse.

Don't forget to keep checking the object information palette to see the data change as you manipulate the object.

Most of the time we don't want to manipulate objects when we click to select them so, by default, keep the "Non Interactive Scaling Mode" button selected as shown in this screengrab.

The third button, "Unrestricted Interactive Scaling Mode" allows the scaling of multiple selected objects. When one of the blue handles is clicked and moved, all the selected objects will move and/or scale together at the same rate.

Remember that we are scaling "objects" here. The lines above are all individual objects but when a series of lines are joined and turned into a new object it will only have selection handles at the corners of the bounding box.

For example, to manipulate the shape of this complex shape we choose the 2D Reshape tool which we will see a little later.

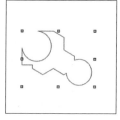

The Selection Tool is the first tool on the Basic

 Tool Palette and is the tool which you should return to by default after you have used any other tool. You will need to select this tool to select objects or multiple objects to either manipulate them and/or read object information in the Object Information Palette.

X is the shortcut for this tool and is one of the keyboard shortcuts which you should definitely learn.

The selection tool has many modes including whether you wish to select objects by drawing rectangles around them (selected in the screen grab below) freehand or just by clicking on the object (default).

Furthermore, as mentioned previously, you must be aware of the first two options in the active toolbar (illustrated below.) "Non Interactive Scaling Mode" and "Interactive Scaling Modes"

The first tool (and the one highlighted above) should be the default as it will allow you to select and move an object without altering it. If you choose the second option, the object, when selected, will have "nodes" allowing you to resize and reshape (in some circumstances). This can be very annoying if you accidently resize your rectangle rather than moving it.

In the screengrab below the first rectangle is selected with Non interactive scaling and the second with Interactive scaling. Note the blue nodes in the right hand picture showing that this one has been selected using the "interactive Scaling Mode"

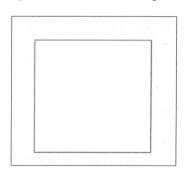 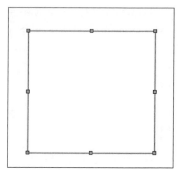

The Pan Tool is another tool which you will use very frequently. When selected It is used to move around your drawing by clicking and holding the mouse button to "grab" the page and move it around. This tool has a very useful shortcut which you should learn. By holding down the spacebar and clicking and holding the mouse button you can move around your drawing in the same way.

 * Some of these tools have a small black triangle at their bottom right. This indicates that there are more tools accessible by clicking and holding the icon. The Pan Tool has a secondary tool called "Move Page Boundary".

This tool allows you to move the page boundary rather then moving the objects on the page. This could be useful if you have started drawing and the drawing has become offset or expanded beyond the page boundary. You will need to have "Show Page Boundary" switched on in the File > Page Setup Menu to use this. Personally I normally don't have the page boundary switched on.

 **The 3D Flyover Tool** is used to view your 3D model from any user-defined angle as if you were flying around it. The "Current View" information box along the top of your screen will read "Custom View" as soon as you use this tool to move away from the predefined views such as Top, Front, Right Isometric, etc.

There are multiple options of "how" you wish to orbit your 3D drawing.

For example by orbiting around the object centre, by a drawing plane or user specified point.

The Zoom Tool does exactly what you would expect, Zooms. There are a couple of options of how you would like to zoom, which become available when you select this tool.

The Text Tool allows you to place text upon your drawing which, of course, is critical for dimensioning and annotating your drawings. It has options as to the style of your text and whether your text is horizontal or angled.

Note also that familiar text options are available such as size, colour, italic, bold, in the text menu in the regular toolbar. These can be applied to any text on your drawing.

The Callout Tool places a block of text attached to a leader line. This is great for additional notes and to add specific information to your drawing. Options include the direction of the leader arrow and the number of points on the line.

Note that to the right of the modes there is a button with a pencil and spanner. This is a preferences button which appears on some tools. When it is clicked it opens up a new window with numerous customisable options for the tool in question. Keep an eye out for this with other tools.

For the callout tool the Preferences button opens up this window but other tools will have very different preferences.

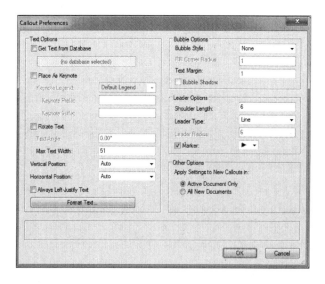

The Locus Tool allows you to place a point on your drawing which can be snapped to and used for reference but will not print on the final drawing.

 Symbol Insertion Tool gives you more options when inserting symbols into walls. This tool will give you lots more options such as offset insertions and how you wish your symbol to be aligned.

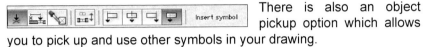 There is also an object pickup option which allows you to pick up and use other symbols in your drawing.

 The Double Line Tool is a really useful tool for drawing two dimensional objects with a thickness, such as stage scenery flattage.

 As you can see there are a number of options within this tool which refer to the line you are drawing, the "Control Line".

For example, if I draw a double line with 200mm spacing left to right with the first "Top Control Line Mode" selected, the thickness of the wall will appear below the line I drew.

The middle option is "Centre Control Line Mode".

And if I do the same with the third "Bottom Control Line Mode" selected the thickness of the wall will be above the line I drew.

Clicking the preferences button will bring up a new box shown overleaf.

Separation is the distance between the lines (in mm).

Control Offset is used in conjunction with the fourth of the control line mode selections (custom control line mode) and defines how much of an offset, from the drawing line, you wish to set.

In the first example below I have drawn two lines 15mm apart using the single line as a reference point. The double lines are drawn from the centre 7.5mm each side of the single line as the control offset is set to 0mm.

In the second example I have set the control offset to 5mm but otherwise drawn the double lines in exactly the same way. You can see now that

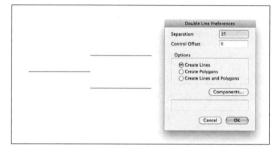

the double lines have been "offset" downwards by 5mm.

The other options in the Preferences box are:

- Create Lines, which creates lines (like in the example above)

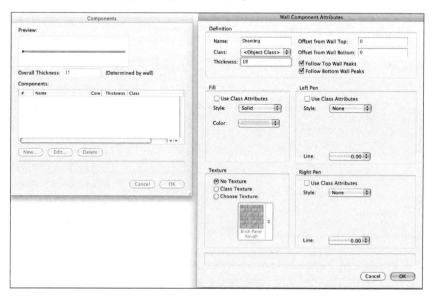

- Create Polygons, which creates enclosed shapes. This is the most likely option when drawing flattage. Creating polygons also allows us to convert the 2D object into a 3D object later on if required.

- Create Lines and Polygons, which does both of the previous. Be careful if you use this as you may end up with stray lines lying on top of your polygons if you don't pay attention.

There is also a "components" button, which allows you to create components of a wall, such as sheeting on top of framing.

In this example I have clicked the Components button, which brought up the box on the left of the diagram below. You can see a preview of my simple 15mm thick wall.

I then clicked "New" to add "components" to my wall. This brought up the dialogue box to the right.

In this box I can create as many components of my wall as I like. Here I have created a "sheeting" component and given it a thickness of 18mm and a nice plywood type colour.

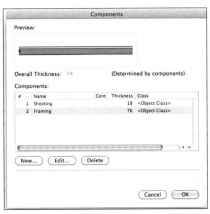

I then click OK and repeat the process with a three inch "framing" component. You can just type 3" into the thickness box, Vectorworks can understand metric and imperial.

You can now see in the preview my new wall consisting of 18mm ply and 3" timber frame. Vectorworks has also calculated my new overall thickness of my wall is 94mm.

You can edit each component part and have the option of lots of different fills to identify the different parts of your drawing. In the screengrab (right) I have chosen "Hatch" from the Fill drop down menu and chosen the "Components Framed Timber" from the options.

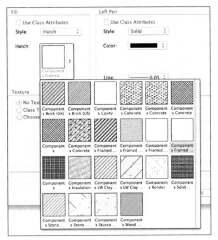

You can create some very detailed drawings using this tool in 2D but the specialised "wall tool" in the building shell toolset is much more powerful and allows simple drawing of hybrid objects which have both 2D and 3D elements.

The Rectangle Tool

This simple tool gives four options

Corner to Corner

Centre to Corner

Centre Side to Corner

Rotated, where the first line defines the angle and the second line the "height"

Use whichever method suits for your drawing.

The Rounded Rectangle Tool

This tool, unsurprisingly, is a rectangle with rounded corners.
There is a preferences button available when you choose this tool which allows you to control the 'roundness' of the corners.

Symmetrical and proportional will give you nice evenly curved corners or you can uncheck those boxes and define your own values for X & Y to make asymmetrical corners.

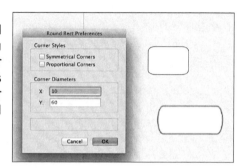

The Circle Tool

As shown in the screengrab (left) there are six tool modes. Each of them are quite obvious by looking at the graphic on the mode button. Make sure you have selected the correct mode when drawing.

The Oval Tool

Ovals are quite simple shapes with only two modes in the toolbar. Oval by drawing a box which defines the extents of the oval or Oval by drawing lines to define height and width.

The Arc Tool

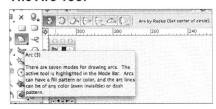

Arcs can be quite complex so take a moment to play around with the seven different modes. Again pay attention to the mode graphic and instructions to the right of the mode buttons. Try out each one, read and follow the instructions.

Be careful with Arcs as they are, by default, filled objects, like slices of a pie. This may not be obvious if your fill colour is set to white and your drawing space is white. To illustrate this, change your fill colour to something pastel as you draw an arc.

If you don't want the filled section, which is quite common, make sure you change the object fill option to none.

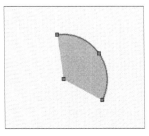

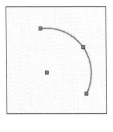

The Freehand Tool

The freehand tools allows you to draw freehand lines.

There is a Preferences button which allows you to set smoothing. This can be a great help if you don't have great mouse skills.

The Polyline Tool

The Polyline Tool is a very commonly used tool, so take a moment to explore all the variables.

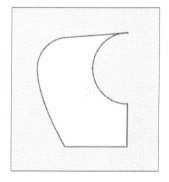

It has six modes for drawing Arcs, curves and lines and a preferences button to change the Fillet Radius (this is only effects the last of the six tools, Fillet Mode).

Remember, you can change between modes mid drawing.

Try to draw something like this as one object and change modes as you draw.

The Polygon Tool

At first look the polygon tool appears to be a simplified version of the Polyline tool but it actually contains a couple of really useful features.

In its default mode it is a simple tool to draw straight sided objects.

However, notice that the icon has a small black triangle in its bottom right hand corner. This tells us that the tool has further options available by clicking and holding the button icon.

When you do so a triangle option appears.

This triangle option allows you to draw equilateral, isosceles and scalene triangles.

First option is "Triangle by Three Sides".

Draw the first side then a preferences box will appear asking for the lengths of each side.

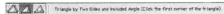

Second option is "Triangle by Two sides and angle".

This time the Preferences box asks for these values.

The third option is "Two Angles and Common Side".

As you can see the preferences box has changed again, asking you to input two angles and a side length.

These options are extremely useful when dealing with drawing triangles.

The Fill Tool

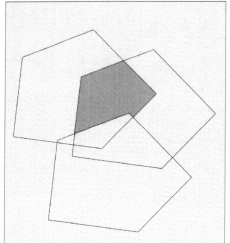

A sub option of the 2D Polygon tool is the Fill Tool. This works in a similar way to that of other programs. Choose the tool and a fill, the cursor into a paint pot, and then click within a boundary to create a new polygon.

You can then move, scale, resize, skew, etc. this polygon as a new object.

The final mode of the Polygon tool is the creation of polygons from an outer boundary.

In this example I have chosen the Polygon From Outer Boundary mode. I have drawn a freehand rough circle, with the tool around my polygons to turn them into a new shape following the outer boundary of my selection.

This is far quicker than selecting all three original polygons, duplicating them and then converting them into a polygon.

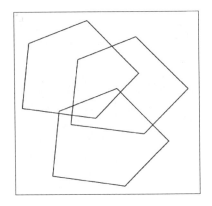

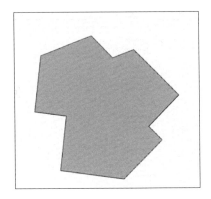

Note that this creates a new polygon, the original is still intact below the new shape.

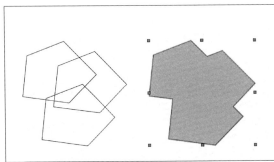

The Double Line Polygon Tool

 This tool is very similar to the double line tool in that you can specify which of the lines in the control line (top, centre, bottom) OR a custom control line mode set through the preferences dialogue.

The Regular Polygon Tool

 This tool allows you to draw polygons with regular sized sides. The number of sides is set in the preferences dialogue box from (3) equilateral triangle upwards.

 Polygons can be drawn from the centre to point, centre to edge or along one edge.

The Spiral Tool

 This odd "basic" tool is one I've never used. It has a number of complex insertion options and a preferences dialogue box where many object parameters can be set.

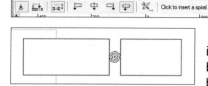

The first insertion option is standard.

The second two options allow you to insert your spiral into a wall...(shown below...no idea why you would do this but there must be a reason)!

The next four icons define the object's insertion point along the X axis and the final, familiar icon opens up a preferences box with lots more options.

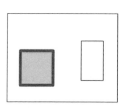

The Eyedropper Tool

This powerful tool can save you lots of time if you have multiple objects with the same attributes.

In this example I have a blue rectangle with a thick red outline and have just drawn a second simple rectangle next to it.

If I click on the eyedropper tool and again on the blue rectangle with red outline, I can "pick up" its attributes (in this case, its blue fill and red outline).

After I have clicked on the left hand rectangle with the eyedropper tool, If I press AND HOLD Cmd on a Mac or Ctrl on a PC, the cursor will change to a paint bucket.

*You can change the icon in the top active toolbar too but the Ctrl function is a really good shortcut to learn.

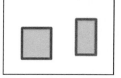

Now, If I click on the right hand rectangle, with the paint bucket cursor it will take on the attributes I picked up from the first one i.e. filled in blue with a thick red border.

To the right of the paint bucket and eyedropper icons on the active toolbar is the familiar Preferences Icon. Clicking this will bring up a new window with a huge number of options. Most of the options are switched on by default but you will see that you have the

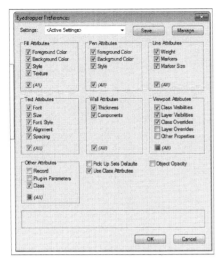

option to be quite specific with which attributes you wish to pick up and put down if your needs are very specific.

The Select Similar Tool

This is another really useful tool with lots of configurable parameters.

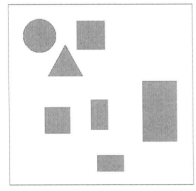

In its default setting, Vectorworks will understand and select "similar" objects on the page.

In this example I have several simple geometric shapes. By selecting the Select Similar Tool and clicking on a rectangle I can see in my object info Pallet that five rectangles have been selected.

If I click on the preferences icon I will see a new box with lots of options, this time with most switched off.

I have changed the settings to "Foreground Colour" and switched off "Object Type".

Using the same example I clicked a blue rectangle.

This time, Vectorworks selects all similar objects according to foreground colour (rather than object type) and displays "7 Objects" in the Object Info Pallette.

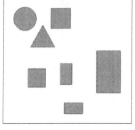

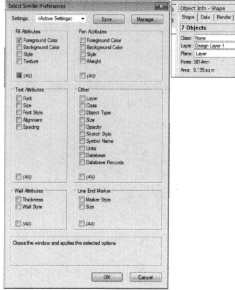

The Visibility Tool

This is another tool I have never used since I normally control class and layer visibility through the Navigation Palette. In the example to the left, the Blue Rectangle Class has been greyed out, and the Green Triangle Class is the active class.

However, this tool allows you to achieve the same by selecting either class or layer from the active toolbar and then whether the class or layer of the next object clicked on is either visible, invisible or greyed out.

The Attribute Mapping Tool

This tool allows you to manipulate hatches, tiles, gradients or image fills.

The screengrab below has a circle with an Aluminium hatch fill. When I select the Attribute Mapping Tool and click on the object I get a rectangle with handles within the hatch which I can then stretch, rotate, etc to get the look I want.

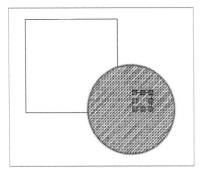
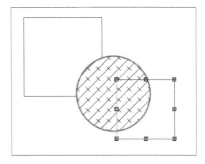

The Reshape Tool

This tools allows modification of polygons and polyline objects by manipulating vertices.

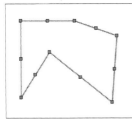

The Screengrab (left) shows a polyline object selected and the Reshape Tool selected.

As you can see the corners and midpoints of each section have been given a blue handle (vertex) which can be dragged to reshape the object.

The tool has a complex array of variables which allow the adding of more vertices, deleting vertices, hiding lines, changing the control point type, different selection methods and adding in fillets. This is a tool you really have to play with to get an idea of what each option does.

Add a fillet (circular arc) vertex to the object.

The Rotate Tool

This tool is fairly self explanatory.

There are only two options, Rotate and Duplicate & Rotate.

As with other tools you must select the object you wish to interact with first and then the Rotate Tool. The first click defines the point around which the object will be rotated and think of the second click as the "handle" by which you will move or reference the rotation.

The Mirror Tool

Again this is a fairly self explanatory tool but somehow manages to cause confusion.

Like the rotate tool, there are only two options, Mirror or Mirror and Duplicate.

The object to wish to mirror must be selected first and then the Mirror Tool slected. You will then be required to draw a line which will indicate the plane of the mirror.

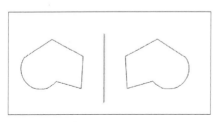

In this example I have the mirror plane to the right of the first object (on the left) and chosen Mirror & Duplicate.

Note that the mirror plane does not have to extend the full length of the "virtual mirror" but only indicate the plane of the mirror.

Also, note that the mirror can exist within the object itself making an overlap when the object is mirrored and duplicated.

I have tried to illustrate both these conditions in the screengrabs below.

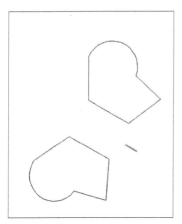

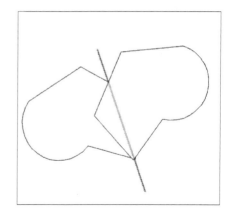

The Split Tool

The split tool can split 2D and 3D Objects.

It has three Options:

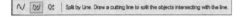

- Point Split
- Line Split
- Line Trim

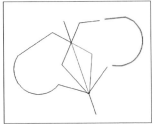

The first option allows you to pick points on the object to determine where the split occurs. In the screengrab (left) I specified two points either side of the Arc on the shape and then used the select tool to select the right hand part of the split and move it away from the original object for clarity.

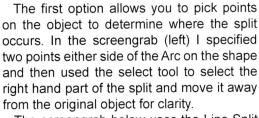

The screengrab below uses the Line Split Option to draw a line through a sphere creating two unequal semi-spheres.

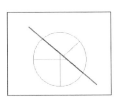

I have moved the sections apart and shaded each half differently for illustration.

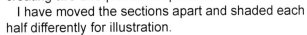

The 3D option is very similar to the Line Split option but gives you an extra Trim option after drawing the intersecting Line where you must define which side of the split you wish to keep. The side you wish to keep is indicated by a small black arrow.

The Connect / Combine Tool

This tool is used to join objects by their endpoints or intersections.

It has four options (don't worry about the preferences button for this tool at this point. It is used specifically for Roof Faces).

- Single Object Connect
- Dual Object Connect
- Dual Object Combine
- Multiple Object Connect

The first option is used to connect an end point to a boundary.

In the screengrab below I have selected the Connect/Combine Tool then clicked on the end of the lower line of the left hand object, then the right hand object. This has extended the line I first selected to extend to meet the second (boundary) object.

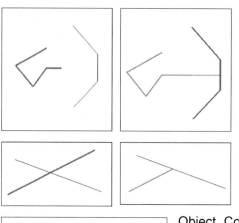

The same tool can also be used "in reverse" to shorten a line back to a boundary instead of extending

In the screengrab below left I have selected the first line as the line I wish to shorten then the second intersecting line as the boundary edge. This has effectively shortened or "trimmed" the first line to the boundary.

The second option "Dual Object Connect" trims or extends two objects to connect them at their endpoints or intersections. Note only "open" objects, such as lines and polylines can be connected. (Except NURBS which we will look at in Chapter 3).

In the screengrab below I have selected the Dual Object Connect Tool and then the end of the left hand shape. The next click extends this line and joins it to the other shape creating a new shape. Note that depending on the position of my second click, Vectorworks will assume the part of the second object I wish to keep.

Furthermore, the Dual Object Connect can be used to quickly extend and connect two endpoints at their intersection.

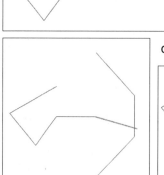

In the screengrab below I have selected Dual Object Connect and then each of the two lines.

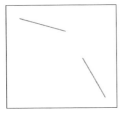
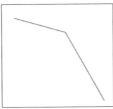

They have been extended by their relative amounts until their intersection where they connect, but still remain as separate lines.

The third Option is almost identical to the Dual Object Connect tool but combines the two objects into a single onject. In the example above the right hand object would become one single object rather than remaining as two joined but separate lines.

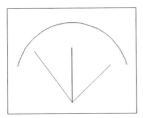

The fourth Option, Multiple Object Connect, trims or extends multiple objects to join a selected boundary object.

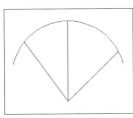

The first click defines the boundary, in this case the curve. The remaining multiple clicks extend or trims those endpoints to the boundary.

The Trim Tool

The Trim tool is relatively straightforward in that it trims a portion of the selected object.

In the screengrab (left) I have drawn a line over one corner of a rectangle. I have then selected the Trim Tool which changes the cursor to a hand icon which is asking you which is the bit to be trimmed. In the screengrab left I have selected the TOP RIGHT of the rectangle (to the right of the cutting line) and then clicked. This has trimmed off the corner of the rectangle using the line as a cutting reference.

Note that if I clicked on the larger part of the rectangle Vectorworks would have taken that as an instruction that the lower left was to be trimmed, leaving the top right section.

Furthermore, If I click on the line itself, Vectorworks will take that instruction that the line is to be trimmed to the intersecting line of the rectangle. The portion of the line clicked will be the piece which is trimmed away.

All three variations are shown below.

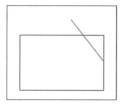 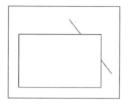 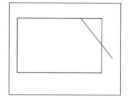

 The Fillet Tool

The fillet tool adds an arc as specified in the preferences options

between two adjacent sides of an object.

There are three tool options as well as the preferences button.

Option one (highlighted above) places a fillet without affecting other objects.

Select the object, then the fillet tool, then I move the mouse over the horizontal and vertical sides of the rectangle they will glow red. Clicking two adjacent sides either places a fillet, as previously defined in the preferences dialogue, or brings up the preferences dialogue box where you are required to specify the fillet radius.

In this example I have drawn a 2000mm X 1000mm Rectangle, then clicked the left and top sides of the rectangle. When the dialogue box appeared I specified a 250mm fillet radius. This placed a fillet on the corner but left the original rectangle intact with the curve/fillet as a separate object.

Option two "Fillet & Split" follows the same sequence but the fillet becomes part of the object and splits the rectangle edges at the intersection of the fillet. In the second screengrab I have moved the

split lines away from the fillet for illustration and clarity.

Option three "Fillet & Trim" removes the corner of the original object completely.

The Chamfer Tool

The chamfer tool is identical to the Fillet tool in the way it is used and behaves.

It has similar options to the Fillet Tool in that you can Chamfer without affecting other objects, Chamfer and Split the lines or Chamfer and Trim.

The only difference is in the options of how you will define the lengths of the chamfer lines.

In the example below I have drawn a rectangle, selected it and then the chamfer tool. I clicked on the two lines which make the top left corner of the rectangle and this options box appears with three data "Entry Options".

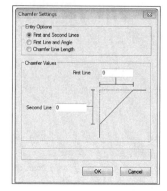

The entry options are fairly self explanatory and the dialogue box is very clear as shown in the screengrabs below.

First & second lines simply ask you to input the lengths of the parts which will be trimmed off the shape.

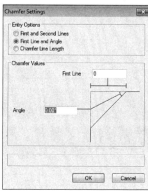

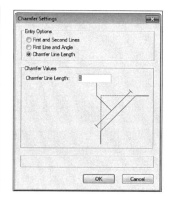

First Line and angle ask you to define the length of a trimmed section and the angle of the second.

Chamfer line length simply asks for the length of chamfer.

The Offset Tool

This is a really useful tool which is used in the "Drawing a Ply Clad Flat" chapter.

The tool has two sets of two options.

Firstly Offset by Distance or Offset by Point.

Secondly, Duplicate and Offset or Offset Original Object.

In this example, I have drawn a rectangle, selected it then the offset tool.

I have chosen Offset by Distance and Duplicate & Offset as in the screengrab above. I have also chosen 32mm as also shown in the screengrab.

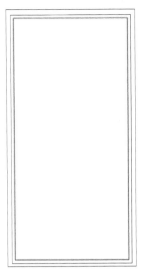

The next mouse click defines whether the rectangle is duplicated inside or outside the original rectangle.

In this example I clicked inside the rectangle to create new rectangle 32mm inside the original.

Just as a word or warning, if you click outside the rectangle to make a new rectangle 32mm outside the original it may appear that the first rectangle disappears. What can happen is that the default "fill" for objects is white and is also the background colour. What has happened is that your new, larger, white filled rectangle, is simply overlaying your original and blocking it out. If you select the new rectangle and choose "Fill" " None" then it will become transparent and you will be able to see the original rectangle again.

The Clip Tool and (Fixed Point Resize / Shear)

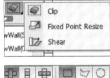

The clip tool is used to cut through an object with a marquee (Rectangle, Polygon, Circle) and there are three clip tools to choose from: Exclusion, Inclusion or Split.

Exclusion (Rectangle) will result in this:

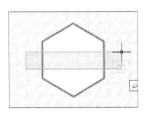

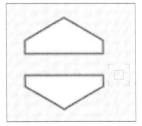

Inclusion (Rectangle) will result in this:

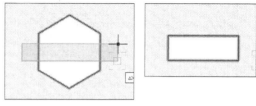

Split (Rectangle) will result in this:

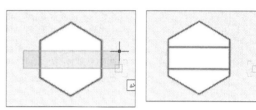

Fixed Point Resize

Fixed point Resize does exactly what you might expect. After selecting the tool it allows you to "pin" one point of the object and resize the rest by dragging the object.

In the screengrab (right) I have pinned the bottom point of the hexagon and resized the shape taller and wider.

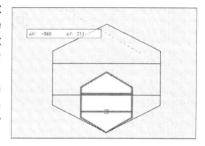

Shear

The shear object is similar to the fixed point resize in that the first click after selecting the tool will "pin" or "fix down" that part of the shape. The next click slects a part of the object to drag and then move the mouse to shear the object.

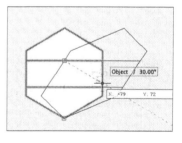

The Move by Points Tool

The Move by Points Tool is extremely useful and has three options as well as a Object Retention toggle button, "number of duplicates" info box and the usual Preferences Box.

Firstly I'm going to click on the Preferences Button, make sure the "Retain Object" button is checked and type 4 into the Number of Duplicates box.

First Option "Move Mode"

Firstly I highlight the object, select the move by points tool then click on a point of the object I wish to use as the reference point (in my example below the bottom point of the hexagon). I then define the direction and distance between this point and the same point of the first duplicated object by either using the mouse or typing into the floating toolbar (In my example I typed in 200mm).

Click the mouse and I have four duplicates who's bottom points are all 200mm apart.

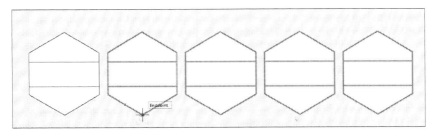

*Because I didn't check the box "Original Object > Leave Selected" in the preferences box above, the original object is now not selected, only the duplicates.

Second Option "Distribute Mode"

Using the same shape and same number of duplicates, this time I will define the TOTAL distance between the reference points rather than define the distance between them.

I click the same bottom point of the shape and then move the cursor out to the right to a defined distance, in this example 500mm.

Click and Vectorworks will evenly add four more shapes between your reference point and your newly defined point.

*dimension added in for clarity.

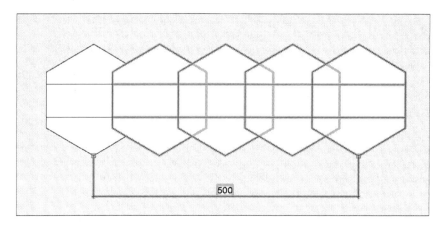

Third Option "Reference Point Mode"

This is a little harder to understand as it will move your object with reference to another. When you select this tool the Duplicates, Object Retention and Preference Dialogue Button all become unavailable.

Simply put, I click a point on my object then a point on another object and tell Vectorworks how far apart those points should be.

I highlight my object select Reference Point Mode, and choose a reference point on the object. (again the bottom point).

I then click a point on another object (this doesn't have to be a point on another object and can be anywhere in space but it's clearer if I use an object for this example).

A pop up box will appear telling me the distance between the two points, asking what I want that distance to be and asking whether the first click was the object or the reference point. In my example it was the object.

So I can type in my new distance e.g. 200mm and change the selection so the first click was the object.

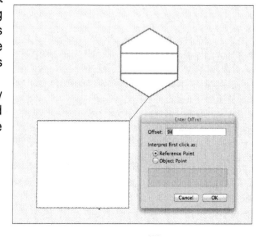

When I click OK the hexagon will move to be 200mm away from the point of the square.

dimension added for clarity. To clarify, the highlighted object will always be the object which moves. The "Define Reference Point or Object Point" selection will depend upon which way you draw the line between the object and the reference point.

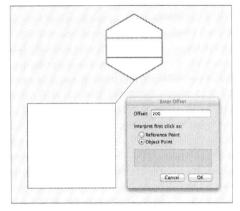

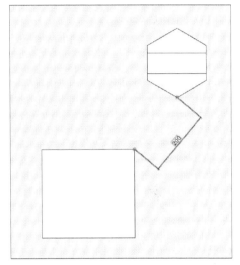

Summary

Those are the tools of the basic tool palette. You will use some of the tools of this palette no matter what your discipline. You may never use some and use others very often but it's worth experimenting a little with each in order to broaden your understanding.

The next chapters will deal with specific examples of theatre and production work. Assumptions will be made that you have a basic understanding of the Basic Tool Palette. Please refer back to this chapter as necessary.

2 DRAWING A PLY-CLAD FLAT

To create a new page navigate to the top menu bar and select File > New.

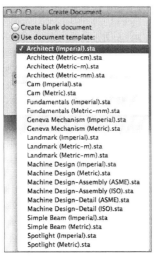

Note that there are options to Use Document Templates. Lots are created for you by default but you can also create your own with, for example, logos, contact information and disclaimers.

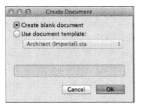

For this chapter we will just select Create Blank Document.

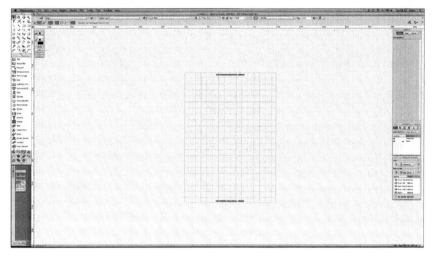

After you click OK you will see a screen which should be very similar to that shown above.

If your workspace looks a little different there may be a few tweaks needed to get it looking like this.

By clicking on Window > Palettes in the menu bar at the top you will see a list of options. The words with a tick next to them are visible palettes.

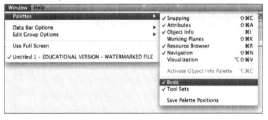

You can click each option to place or remove a tick and therefore make the palette visible or not.

Make sure yours looks the same as in the screengrab (left).

These palettes are floating and may be dragged around and resized to suit your screen and working preference. You may have noticed that there is a "save palette positions" at the bottom of the drop down list. Use this when you are happy with the position and size of the palettes. When you run Vectorworks again the palettes will be in the same position.

The next thing to change, before we start drawing, Is to get rid of the grid.

This is just personal preference and the grid is certainly a powerful tool which I will cover later. For this exercise however we wont be using it.

Double click on the button that looks like a grid in the "Snapping" palette.

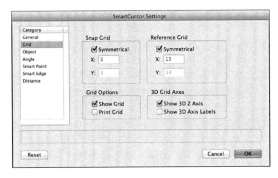

This will open up a new window.

You can switch off the grid by clicking the tick box "show grid" button to remove the tick.

Notice, the options to "Snap Grid" and "Reference Grid". These can be very useful in the future.

Before we start I'll just explain a couple of basic concepts.

The screen in front of you is a working space where we will build up our drawing. This is NOT the space where we will set print views, decide on scale, paper size or anything to do with final presentation (whether paper or digital).

This is a really important concept to remember and if you do keep that in mind it will make the later 3D chapters much clearer.

We will set the scale, associated paper size and print options later, once we have drawn our object. Therefore, since we have a limitless virtual workspace we will work 1:1 (or without scaling). We don't need to consider scale at the moment, only when we wish to represent out object on a known paper size do we need to consider scale.

There is a handy scale icon in centre of the top tool bar and this should be set to 1:1 to keep things nice and simple.

If you don't have this icon then click on the little black arrow to the furthest right of your toolbar.

This will bring up a drop down box which lists all the active toolbar components. Make sure there is a tick next to "Layer Scale".

We are going to draw a ply clad flat.

This consists of a wooden frame, a large sheet of plywood and some corner plates, which help keep it nice and rigid.

A small version of the final drawing is shown overleaf.

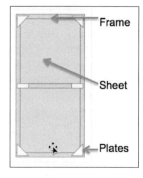

We are nearly ready to start drawing but before we rush in and start lets define some "classes".

Classes are just a way of grouping things. This can allow us to select those groups and give characteristics to them. In this example the colour of the plates is different to the frame so that we can see them easily.

Therefore, Instead of having to assign a colour each time we draw a plate we tell Vectorworks to make everything in the "plates class", yellow, everything in the "frame class" tan and everything in the "sheet class" green.

Classes can be much more powerful than this but this is just a basic example of their use.

So lets set up classes for the frame, plates and sheet.

Click up top left in the toolbar on the little icon left of the word "none".

This will open a new window, The Organisational Palette, showing us the classes within the document.

There are two classes which will always be present in a new drawing, they are "Dimension" and "None". All objects will be assigned to the "none" class by default unless assigned to another class. All dimensions are assigned to the dimension class by default unless assigned to another class.

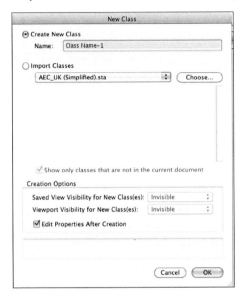

These two classes cannot be deleted.

Click, "New..." and this will give us the option to create a new class (left).

The little button next to "Create New Class" should be on (if it's not click it to switch it on), and the "Class Name" should be highlighted. Type, "Flat-Frame" in the box then making sure "Edit Properties After Creation" is ticked down the bottom (it should be by default), and click OK.

We now get an Edit Classes box shown left.

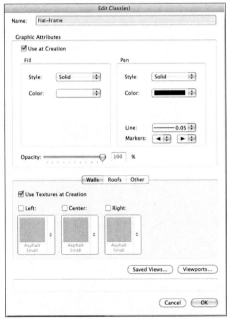

Put a tick in the "Use at Creation" box which is near the top, just below the where you have named your new class.

Now select a colour by clicking the white box to the right of the word "colour".

If you only have black and white colours in your colour palette then don't be disappointed, this just means that the colour palette is showing the colours in the "Active Document" of which, at the moment, there is only black and white.

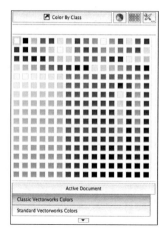

To expand the selection to a full colour palette click on one of the two rectangular buttons at the bottom of the colour window which say "Classic Vectorworks Colours" or "Standard Vectorworks Colours".

This will bring up a lovely selection of colours. (Choose something pastel just so your drawing doesn't become too garish.)

If you want to experiment with more colours then click the preferences button at the top right of the palette to show a huge range of colour palettes including ROSCO TV & Scenic Paints (below).

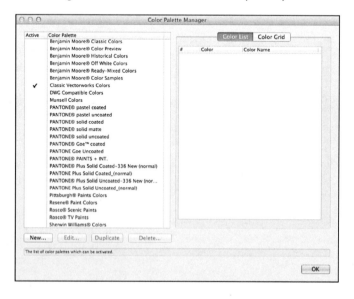

By selecting and placing a tick next to a palette in this list it will then be available as a rectangular button at the bottom of your colour palette for quick selection.

Choose a colour, Click OK and your new class will be created.

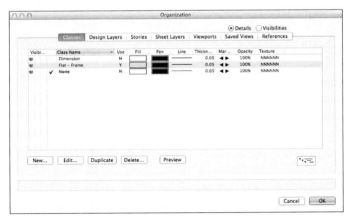

The colour you picked will now be associated with anything which you define as being in that class. (This will become apparent later if that doesn't make sense).

Do this again creating classes for:

"Flat-Plates"

"Flat-Sheet"

Type these exactly as shown (without the quotes). The hyphen is important, as it will help the organisation of your classes. In this drawing we will have a class called "Flat" and within it a subclass of "Frame", "Plates" and "Sheet".

You should have something within your Organization window, under the Classes Tab which looks something like the image shown right.

If you have a newer version of Vectorworks the classes will already be nested together under the "Flat" class.

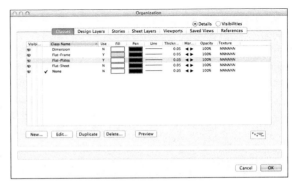

Now to start drawing

Our flat will be 1220mm by 2440mm since this is the size of a single piece of plywood. This is very close to 4ft by 8ft. Vectorworks is very clever and we can input dimensions in either imperial or metric (or even a mixture of both). On this occasion though we'll stick to mm.

 Choose the rectangle tool and draw an 1220 x 2440 rectangle in the middle of the page using the corner to corner mode. (Tip: start drawing it from the bottom left corner). Input the

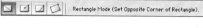

dimensions directly into the floating toolbar by simply typing 1220, then use the TAB key (left of Q) to move from the X dimension to the Y then type 2440 then press Return/ Enter TWICE on the keyboard to finish. (You can mouse click to finish but any movement of the mouse will overrule the data you have just entered.)

This rectangle will eventually become the plywood sheet with a thickness of 4mm. Think of it as lying on the workshop floor and we are looking down on it (Top/Plan View).

Now to add some framing.

Before we go on, make sure that "Snap to Object" and "Smart Points" are selected in the Snapping

Palette. This will allow us to line up the corners of the framing with the sheet.

We are now going to draw the BOTTOM rail using the rectangle tool, which is 1220 wide, the same as the sheet and 70mm high (or a 4' length of 3"x1" timber if you prefer).

Make sure the rectangle tool is still selected and then Click the bottom LEFT corner of the rectangle and start drawing a rectangle. Since we have snapping turned on we will just free hand the horizontal dimension in a second. Press TAB TWICE (Once to select the X dimension in the floating toolbar, which we have just said we will freehand, and the second time to select the Y dimension). Type 70 into the Y dimension in floating toolbar and a red dotted line will appear showing the one dimension you have defined.

Using the mouse to just freehand over right and "snap" to the point where the red line dotted intersects with the frame.

It should now look like the picture below.

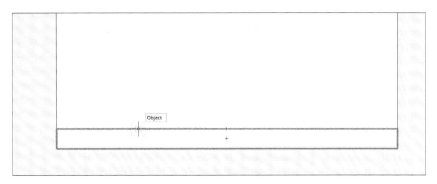

There a multiple ways to do this in Vectorworks. Once you have completed this tutorial you should try a few more like drawing the rail as a separate rectangle 70mm by 25mm outside the rectangle and dragging it in to snap within the shape. See if you can find any more.

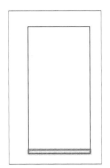

Next we want to draw the top rail (which could be done by adapting the method we have just used) but for this exercise we will use the mirror and duplicate tools.

Make sure the bottom rail is selected and "glowing" orange (as in my screengrab above) then select the Mirror Tool from the Basic Tool Palette.

This tool allows us to place a virtual mirror on the page and if the "Mirror AND Duplicate" option is selected it will duplicate the selected object.

With the mirror tool selected and the bottom rail highlighted, draw a line (a virtual mirror) horizontally across the centre of the rectangle and, assuming you have drawn your mirror exactly central, your top rail will appear perfectly in place.

Note that you don't need to draw the "mirror" the whole way from side to side of the rectangle either, even just the centre to the edge is fine. (In

fact the mirror line doesn't need to be anywhere near the drawing, it's just a reference line but, for now, think of it as placing a mirror vertically as you are looking down on your drawing).

Now we will draw the sides of the frame and will use a different method just for practice.

Choose the Rectangle Tool (Corner to Corner) and just start drawing a rectangle from bottom left to top right. Type 70 into the floating toolbar for the X Dimension (for the 3" width of the frame timber).

For the Y dimension we need to ask Vectorworks to do a little bit of maths for us. We know that the length of this piece of wood will be 2440mm MINUS 70mm from the top rail and 70mm from the bottom rail (so that it sits inside the top and bottom rails).

Instead of doing the maths on a calculator press TAB to highlight the Y dimension and just type 2440-70-70 into the floating toolbar. (I know you could have worked out 2440-140 but I'm just showing you that you can type maths straight into the floating toolbar.) Press Return twice on the keyboard to finish.

You should now have a 70 by 2300 rectangle sitting outside the original rectangle.

Choose the Select Tool.

(Non Interactive Scaling Mode)

Select the new rectangle by the top left (or bottom left) corner and move it into position within the flat. If the snap options are still on, the rectangle should snap into position.

Close up Image and full flat images for reference.

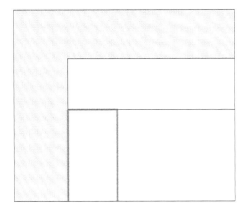

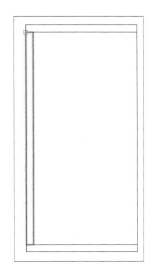

Use the Mirror Tool again to create the other vertical stile.

We now only have the centre rail to draw into place and the frame will be complete.

Let's use a different tool to draw this to give you more practice with various methods.

Choose the Double Line Tool.

Then click the "centre control line mode" and then the preferences button.

When you click the Preferences Button a new window will pop up asking for some information.

Make sure the separation distance is set to 70mm (since that's the 3" width of the timber).

We also want to create a polygon i.e. a rectangle, so make sure

Create Polygons is selected as in the screengrab left and click OK.

Assuming the "Snap to Object" and "Smart Points" are still active in the "Snapping" Palette, all you need to do is hover your mouse over the centre of the right hand side of the left hand stile and you will be able to snap to the centre point.

Draw your rectangle from the left to the right and snap again to the centre point of the opposite stile as in the picture below.

We now need to select the entire flat.

Choose the select tool.

Draw a selection box around the whole flat from top left to bottom right. It should look like the screengrab below. The glowing orange indicates it has been selected and the Object Information Palette (top right) should say "6 Objects".

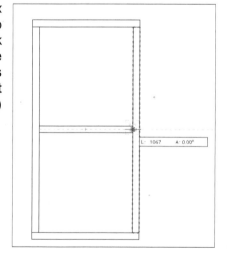

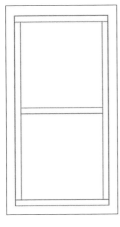

You'll notice that along with the information stating that "6 Objects" have been selected, the "Class" is set to "None". Remember we defined a class for the frame, so now it's time to tell Vectorworks that these objects are our "Flat-Framing" and they will take on the characteristics of the class as defined earlier. We'll alter the sheet object in a moment.

With the six objects of the frame still selected simply click the drop down arrow to the right of the word "none" in the Object Information Palette. This will show us the classes as defined, and then

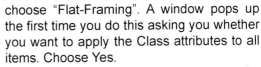

choose "Flat-Framing". A window pops up the first time you do this asking you whether you want to apply the Class attributes to all items. Choose Yes.

You'll notice that the "Flat" Class has the three subclasses within it. This is because when we created the classes we used a hyphen after the word "Flat" to define a top category and then defined sub categories after the hyphen. This may not seem to make a lot of sense in this example but it's really good practice and helps a lot when you have a big drawing with lots of classes.

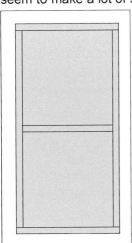

You're probably looking at your drawing and thinking something went wrong at this point since it looks like the screengrab left.

Also the mathematicians among you will have been wondering how three horizontals and two verticals equals six objects.

This is because we selected everything when we drew a selection box around our drawing, including the first 1220mm x 2440mm rectangle we drew.

This original 2440 x 1220 rectangle is the sheet and we created a Class for the sheet.

Now, select the original rectangle by clicking inside its area. Make sure only the rectangle is

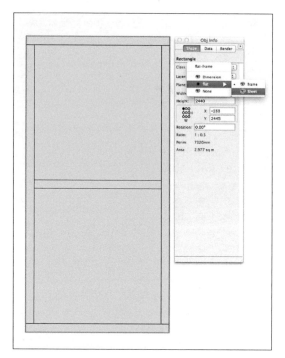

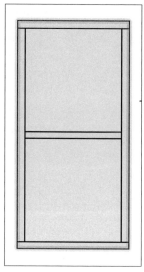

selected. The Object Info Palette should only say "Rectangle". If this is the case then change its class to "Flat-Sheet".

Your drawing should look a little better now that the framing and sheet colour attributes of the class have been associated to the correct parts of the drawing.

Now let's draw in the plates.

Firstly we will define a new rectangle which will act as our guide for lining up the plates. We will set this rectangle 32mm smaller than the sheet. This allows space for the frames to sit together when the flat is constructed if butted together in a 90 degree corner.

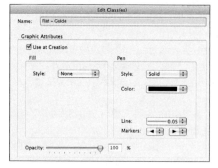

Before we do anything else we're going to create another Class called "Flat-Guide". Set its attributes as the screengrab left.

Make sure the Fill Style is set to "None".

Now to draw the guide rectangle.

Make sure only the original rectangle, our "Flat-Sheet" is selected. (It's good practice to check in the Info Pallette which should say "Rectangle".)

Then choose the Offset tool from the basic tool palette and make sure the "Offset by Distance" and "Duplicate & Offset" are checked.

Also, change the number in the Distance Box to 32.

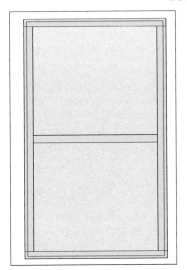

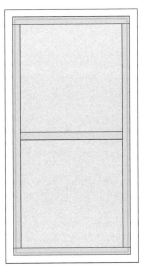

Very carefully (assuming the rectangle is selected) click once inside the original framing rectangle and Vectorworks will duplicate another rectangle 32mm inside it. Your new rectangle will be selected and remain highlighted as long as you don't click anything else.

Now, change its class to Frame-Guide and then while it is still highlighted go to the Modify Menu on the top bar and choose "Send to Front". This will bring the outline of our new guide rectangle to the "front" or "top" of the drawing.

We now have our guide to place the final plates.

 Choose the Polygon tool and click the "Snap to Angle" icon in the snapping Palette.

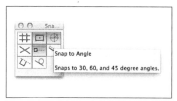

This will allow us to snap to 45° when we draw the corner plates.

Click the top left corner of the Guide Rectangle and move your cursor to the right. The floating toolbar will appear and you can type in 200 to define the length of that side. A red dotted circle will appear showing you all the points

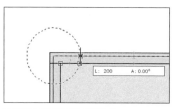

200mm from your first click. Click again along the guide line horizontally (or if the line is already there just hit return or enter on the keyboard.

Move your mouse down and left and (providing the snap to angle has been enabled) you should be able to snap to

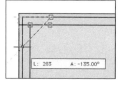

-135 °.

The degrees in many CAD programmes work the same way, 0° at three o'clock to 180° at nine o'clock working anti-clockwise through 12 o'clock. Working clockwise it works round in minus figures through six o'clock.

Click on the guide line when the A: (angle) reads -135° then up and click again at the corner where you started. This will create a triangle polygon.

All that's left now is to change its Class to "Flat-Plates" and it will take on the colour you defined when you created the "Flat-Plates" Class.

Use the Mirror tool to place the other three corner plates (or draw them for practice).

For the Centre Rail plates choose the Double Line tool. Set the Separation to 70mm and the Centre Control Line Mode.

Click on the Centre Snap Point of the guide rectangle and start drawing the plate. When the floating toolbar appears type in 200mm.

Use the Mirror Tool again to set the opposite side.

Your Flat should be complete.

The only thing now is to remove the guide rectangle.

If you are sure you wont need it again you can select it and delete it.

Alternatively you can hide the guide by hiding the "Flat-Guide" Class.

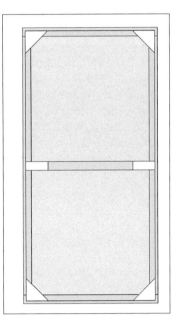

In the Navigation Window (to the right) you will be able to see your classes.

The little eye symbol in the left hand column sets the Visibility of the Class. It can be either Visible, Invisible, or Greyed.

Click in the second Column next to Flat-Guide to place an X in the Column and make the Class Invisible.

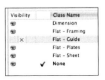

As a final note The Tick defines the Active Class. You can click in this column to select items within the class. Be aware though that when a Class is Active it is visible so if you find you have made a class invisible but you can see it, just check that the Class isn't Active.

The final 2D drawing is shown, right.

We could leave our drawing like this or put some dimensions on it and it would be a useful piece of technical drawing.

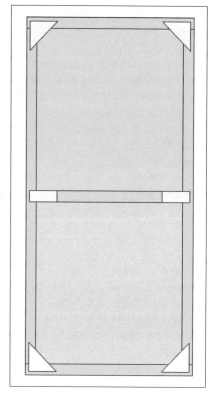

But let's turn it 3D.

Firstly we need to control how we select and manipulate the Classes.

We have our objects correctly assigned to classes but for this part of the exercise we only want to select the objects within each specified class as we convert each of them in turn into 3D objects.

So, we need to look again at the Navigation Palette and change the Class Options from "Show/Snap/Modify Others" to "Show/Snap Others" by clicking on the words "Show/Snap/Modify Others" to reveal a dropdown list where you should choose "Show/Snap Others".

This will allow us to make a class active (like the "Flat-Plates" class in the screengrab) right and select all objects in that class without affecting the other classes.

Select the "Flat-Frame" Class by clicking to the left of the words. A tick should appear indicating that is the active class.

Make sure nothing is selected, then with the selection tool, draw a box around the whole flat. Only the Framing should get selected.

You can check if this has worked by looking in the Object Info palette to see that only five objects within the "Flat-Frame" Class have been selected.

Then choose Model > Extrude from the Top Menu and type 25 into the "Extrusion" since the timber is 25mm thick.

This effectively pulls up all the framing rectangles 25mm and creates 3D Objects.

Don't worry that the objects appear to vanish or lose their colour. This is because the colour fill only applied to the 2D line drawing. Now the object is 3D we treat it differently and it's colour will only show when rendered.

I can check to see that this has worked by choosing one of the Isometric Views from the top toolbar.

Here I can see that the framing clearly now has a three dimensional element to it. It's worth noting at

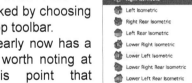

this point that Vectorworks 2015 comes with the option of defining how your 3D render mode and projection will look. By default it may be set up to be Open GL render and "normal perspective".

I prefer my drawing to remain in

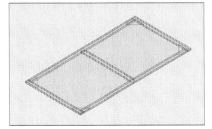

Wireframe until I decide to render it and also prefer it to be shown in Orthogonal projection. I can change these settings in Vectorworks > Preferences > 3D tab. You can change this or leave it but your 3D views may look a little different to my sceengrabs if you are set to Open GL & Normal Perspective.

Return to the Navigation Palette and select "Plates".

This allows you to select all the "Flat-Plates" classed objects in the drawing and extrude them to 6mm.

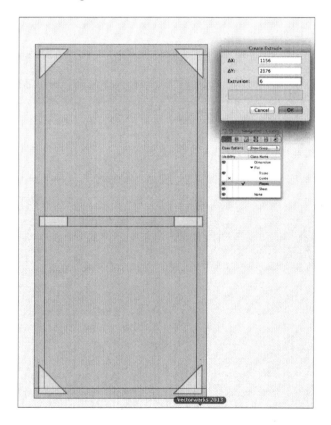

And lastly select the original rectangle, the "Flat-Sheet" and extrude to 4mm.

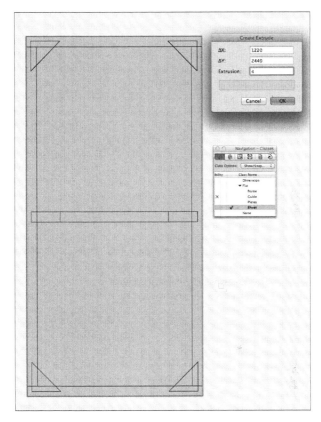

Remember to deselect previously selected objects before each step.

By now all the lovely colours will have vanished from your drawing, but don't worry, it'll look even better very soon.

 Click on the Flyover Tool and have a spin around your 3D flat. It's all there in 3D but not stacked correctly.

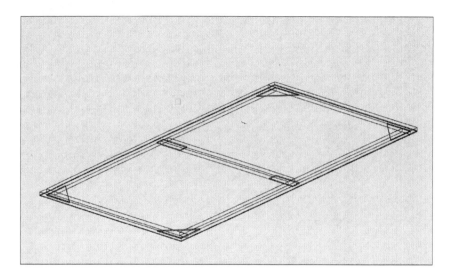

If we assume it's lying face down then the sheet will be on the floor, the framing sitting on the sheet and the plates sitting on the framing.

We can do this visually but it's better to do it accurately by just setting the known distances from the floor. Remember Vectorworks can do the Maths for you if you're not 100% confident.

Go back to the Top/Plan View by selecting it from the Top Toolbar.

Go back to the Navigation Palette, make sure the "Flat-Sheet" Class is selected, and with the selection tool, draw a selection rectangle round the entire flat to just select the sheet.

Look at the Object Info Pallette.

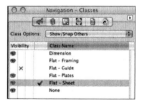

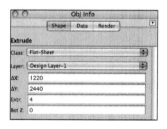

You can see that the Bot Z: value is 0, this means it is sitting in the "floor".

Choose the "Flat-Framing" Class and select the frame components on the drawing. Notice it is also sitting on the floor. We know it should be sitting on the 4mm sheet so change the value in the Bot Z: to 4.

Do the same with the "Flat-Plates". Remember these sit on the 25mm frame which in turn sits on the 4mm sheet. So you can type in 29 as the Bot Z value (or "4 + 25").

*Remember you actually have to select the class items in the drawing each time and again, don't forget to deselect each step or you'll end up with multiple class selections.

You should now have a completed 3D flat.

In the top toolbar there is a dropdown menu to allow you to view your drawing from many standard angles.

Note there is a distinction between Top and Top/Plan.

2D drawings can only be viewed in Top/Plan. The Top view is to view 3D drawings from the top.

Click a couple of the other views to see your flat from different angles.

Just to the right of the "Views" dropdown choices is the render button (which is a teapot) and lots of render choices.

Currently it will be set to "Wireframe".

Click on "OpenGL", which is a fast render, and you will see your creation as a fully rendered 3D object (below).

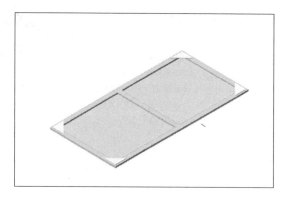

Experiment with other renders.

3 WORKING IN 3D

The 3D Toolset has a number of predefined 3D objects which help speed up 3D modelling. In this section we will just use basic 2D shapes and extrude them in order to keep the process clear. However, the processes can be used on any solid 3D object.

Go to Top/Plan View.

Draw a rectangle 1000 x 500.

Now go to Model > Extrude to 200.

Draw a Circle 700 diameter and extrude to 300mm.

Note that when you extrude the 2D shape the view changes to Top rather than Top/Plan. This is because Top/Plan is a 2D only view and therefore when you create a 3D object it should be viewed in the 3D "Top" View.

Your shapes should look similar to my screengrab right.

If you are using Vectorworks 2015 and your view looks different to my screengrab then navigate to View > Projection and change the setting to Orthogonal.

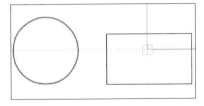

The next step is to use these two basic shapes to create a more complex shape by merging them together.

Move one of the shapes over the other so they overlap.

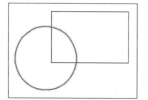 Select BOTH objects.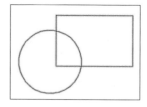

Then go to Model > Add Solids.

This will combine your two objects into a single 3D object.

 Change the view to Right Isometric and give your object a quick render and it should look something like this.

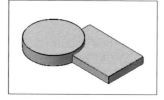

Let's do the same thing again from scratch but try the other options within the Model menu such as Subtract, Intersect & Section Solids.

When you select Subtract Solids from the menu you will be asked for an additional piece of information. Vectorworks will ask you which of the two objects is "the object".

Vectorworks will normally have a good guess but you can manually select which of the objects you have overlapped to be the object and which will therefore be the cutter by pressing the arrows in the option window to make sure the object is highlighted red.

In this example the circle will be the object and the rectangle will be the cutter.

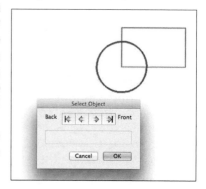

In this example the rectangle is 200mm high but the cylinder 300mm. Therefore the rectangle has cut a section out underneath leaving a 100mm "top" on the cylinder.

This Lower Right Isometric shows the shape from below.

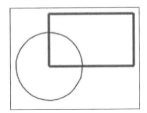

Let's run the same Subtract Solids command again but this time change the "object" to the rectangle.

We can see that this creates a very different result.

Let's try the Intersect option now.

With both objects selected the tool simply creates a new object made from the overlapping section of the two objects.

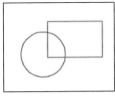

The final selection in this menu is the Section Solids option but we won't deal with this just now as it won't be obvious on such a simple object.

Once you have created your 3D models you can manipulate them as you would a 2D drawing.

Within the 3D Tool Set is a tool called Push/Pull. This should be familiar with anyone who has used Google's 3D Modeling Software. By selecting this tool you can grab a face of an object and push or pull it to change its properties.

Go back to your 3D object in Isometric View and choose the Push/Pull tool.

As your mouse cursor hovers over your object it will highlight each face. When the face you wish to manipulate is highlighted simply click to select that face.

You can then "pull" (or push) the face you have chosen to manipulate the shape. You will notice the floating toolbar is

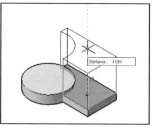 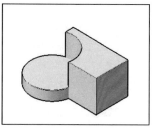

also present allowing you to input dimensions numerically.

Let's suppose you now want to place a 3D Pentagon on the top of your newly extracted object. If you switch back to Top/Plan view and draw then extrude your object will be sitting at "ground level" or Z 0 and be "inside" your 3D model.

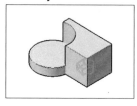

You could, if you knew the height of the object you are placing your pentagon on simply change the Z height of your pentagon to set its base at that height.

Or switch to front and side view and manually move the new pentagon into position but this can be tricky.

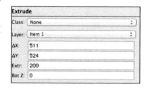

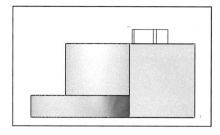 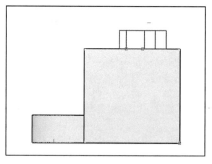

There is an easier way using the "set working plane" tool.

Go back to your model and select Right Isometric View.

Click the "Set Working Plane" Tool in the 3D Modeling Toolset.

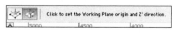

Make sure the "Planer Face Mode" is selected as in the screengrab below left.

Now move your mouse pointer over your 3D model and Vectorworks will highlight the planar faces as your cursor moves over them. When the tool has highlighted the top face of the object, click to set the working plane.

We now want to name this working plane by clicking "Add" in the Working Planes Palette.

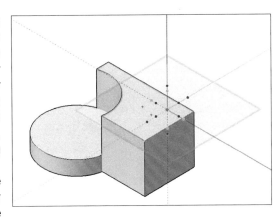

We can call this anything we like and click OK.

Now go back to "Top View" and select the working plane we have just defined here in the top menu bar.

You should now be looking down on a plan view of your object but with a working plane set on top of the object rather than the default Z0 or ground level. You can now draw and extrude your pentagon directly in place.

Choose the Regular Polygon and define the number of sides as 5 in the tool preferences.

Draw and extrude your pentagon in top view to 500mm then change to Isometric View to see the results.

This technique of setting working planes is really useful.

Practice the method by drawing a small cylinder from one of the sides of the pentagon. It should only take a minute.

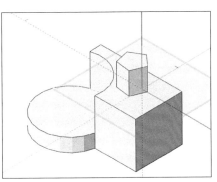

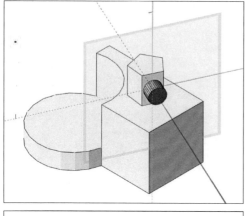

One of the 3D commands I have used a lot is the Model > Extrude Along Path.

I have used this in the creation of scaffolding tubes, curved brass rails in a theatre auditorium and a complex catwalk structure in a studio. The command is quite simple and uses a "profile" 2D object with a "path" object.

First draw a 48mm DIAMETER circle, (the diameter of standard scaffold tube) then draw a 2000mm line.

Make sure both are selected as in the screengrab above.

Select the Model > Extrude Along Path option and Vectorworks will ask you which of the shapes is the path.

In this example the path is the 2000mm line so make sure that is selected (glowing red) and press OK. You can change which object is selected by using the arrow keys marked <<Prev and Next>>.

Assuming you have extruded a 48mm circle along a 2000mm line you will have created a 48mm virtual 3D scaffold tube for you to add to your design or convert to a "lighting position". (see the Spotlight chapter).

You will notice there are several other options within the Extrude Along Path options box such as

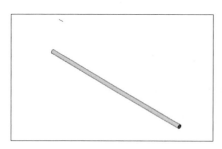

"Uniform Scale" and "Exponential Scale".

In this example I have extruded the same 48mm circle along the same 2000mm line but given it a **Uniform Scale** of 3 creating a long conical object which has a diameter at the right hand side three times that of the original circle.

In the example below I have selected the **Exponential Scale** option and again given it a scale factor of 3. This time I have created a flared trumpet type object. Experiment and remember you can still alter and manipulate any of these objects after creation.

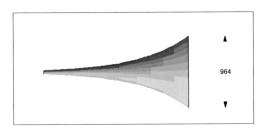

Scale Objects

The Modify > Scale Objects tool is really useful in a variety of situations. I will demonstrate a couple of uses below.

Firstly I will use the trumpet like Exponential Extrude I have just created.

I have returned to Wireframe Render and Top/Plan view for clarity.

First, make sure the object is selected.

We know the right hand side of the object is dimensioned at 964mm so I will use the Scale Objects command to quickly change this to 900mm.

Choose Modify > Scale Objects and you will be presented with an options box like this.

Click on the scale by distance Icon here.

The box will disappear and you will be back in the drawing again seemingly as though nothing has happened. However, Vectorworks is now

waiting for you to draw a line over a known dimension, in our case the right hand end of the object.

Draw a line down the vertical known edge of the object as you would drawing any line. Click at the top, then the bottom and Vectorworks will then present you with the dialogue box again.

We can see that there is a "current distance" dialogue box showing 964mm (the line or distance we have just specified) and a box beneath it asking what the New Distance should be.

Type 900 into this New Distance box. This tool effectively says, "scale this size, which is currently 964mm down to 900mm".

When you click OK, the selected object will be resized to meet the parameters you have just specified.

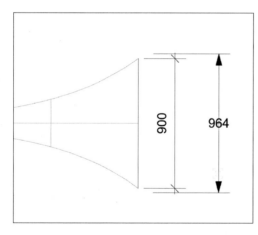

Use the linear dimension tool or the tape measure tool to confirm.

Please remember that this has scaled the whole selected object. Therefore the left hand side is no longer 48mm. If you need to create a 48mm to 900mm exponentially curved trumpet you will need to use different tools. This is just a demo of "Scale Object".

Let's return to the previous question of creating a trumpet like object with a 48mm small end and 900mm large end.

There are a number of ways to do this which will illustrate the variety of approaches to 3D modelling.

The following method will involve creating a "slice" of the object and then "sweeping" it round 360°.

I have quickly drawn a segment of the object using lines and a curve. (think of it as a slice of a chocolate orange).

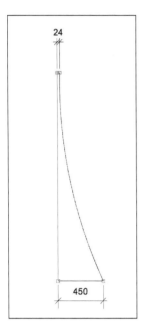

(I've added dimensions just for clarity.)

We now need to convert this shape (which is currently just a group of lines) into a "surface" (one object with an area rather than four lines).

Select the whole object then Modify > Combine into Surface.

Use the Fill Tool and click within the shape. This "fills" the shape and creates an object with an area. The Object Info palette will confirm the four lines have now become a "Polyline".

Note: If there is any break or gaps within your drawing this will not work. Take care to make

sure that the lines of your original drawing are joined up properly.

Also be aware that the original line drawing will still exist "underneath" your new Polyline. You can simply move the new Polyline and delete the original line drawing.

Now, make sure your Polyline is selected and choose Model > Sweep.

A dialogue box will appear.

The height and Radius have been read from your drawing. The only section you need to think about is the Arc Angle. In this case I want to completely sweep round 360° to make a solid object. If you only needed a half shape or three-quarters of a shape you can alter the sweep here.

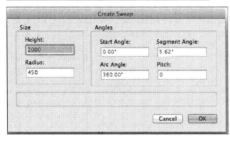

Keep the data as in the screengrab (left), we can click OK and the object will be created.

I've given the object a nice purple Open GL render and added dimensions to prove that the objects meet the criteria

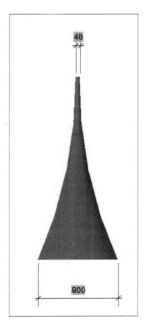

noted at the beginning of the example.

Hopefully you now have a basic understanding of some of the 3D tools available to you in Vectorworks. By using the Add & Subtract Solids commands, and the Extrude along Path and Sweep commands you can create a huge number of complex 3D objects. Combine this with proper use of Working Planes and you will have a powerful 3D modelling tool at your disposal.

NURBS

Within the 3D Tools palette is the NURBS Curve tool.

Since NURBS are different to the 3D solid objects we have been

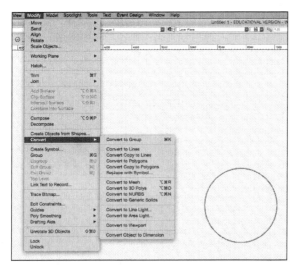

looking at in this chapter it's worth taking a moment to understand what NURBS are and how they can be used.

NURBS are Non Uniform Rational Bezier Splines.

They are useful for creating more organic shapes and can be bent, pulled and stretched using U and V degree vertices.

Any 2D polyline,

Arc, Circle, etc can be converted into a NURB by selecting the 2D object, then Modify > Convert to NURBS.

In this example a circle has been converted to a NURBS object. We can see this by the info in the Object Info Palette.

The interesting aspect of NURBS is that although they are essentially 2D they can have a position in 3D space. Note the Z value in the screengrab right.

Try this very simple exercise in which we will create a NURBS "surface" from a simple 2D object.

Draw a rectangle, then choose Model > 3D Power Pack > Create Surface from Curves.

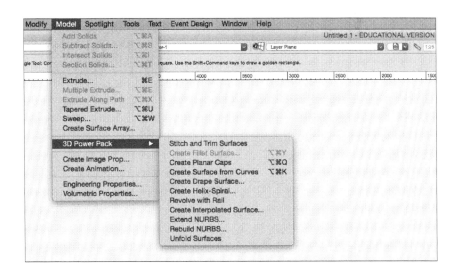

I know the "curves" terminology may be a little off-putting as our rectangle is four straight lines.

Check in the Info Pallette and our Rectangle should now says "Nurbs Surface".

The U Degree and V Degree info boxes determine how many Horizontal and Vertical sections the surface is divided into.

Change the values to 2 and 2 to create nine vertices and check the "show vertices" box.

The great thing with Nurbs is that I can now shape this "sheet" as if it were a soft, highly pliable surface.

If I choose the Rehape tool in the basic tool palette I can begin
to push and pull any of the vertices of the object.

There are options within the Object Info Pallette to move
individual vertices, or all those in the U or V plane.

So I have chosen Vertex Only, meaning I only
wish to move one point at a time.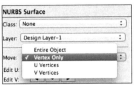

I can select the Vertex I wish to move by using
the Edit U and Edit V buttons in the Object Info
Palette.

Pressing the dot (between the two arrows)
will flash the particular Vertex that is currently
selected in the object. The arrows to the left and
right can be used to select the Vertex that you
intend to move.

Once the cursor is over the live Vertex then
it will change to a small box with four arrows.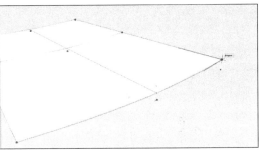

The edges of the object
nearby will also glow
red. This indicates that
the object is ready to be
reshaped.

I have reshaped the
rectangle slightly in the
screengrab right.

NURBS can also be
used to create theatrical
soft goods.

Draw a gentle curve using the NURBS curve tool in the 3D Tool Palette
in Top View. Mine is around 2500mm long.

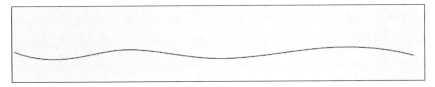

This will be the bottom of the curtain.

I now want to duplicate this shape and give it a height which will be the
top of the curtain.

I have "Offset Duplications" turned on by default but in this case it wont be helpful as I want the top of the curtain to be exactly on top of the bottom in the Z plane.

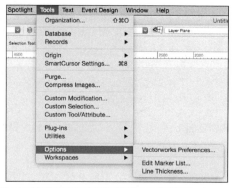

I could duplicate and then drag it back over and snap it to the original but in this case I'll unselect the "offset duplications" to show you that this option can be useful depending on workflow.

Choose Tools > Options > Vectorworks Preferences.

Then uncheck the "Offset Duplications" option (third option on the left hand side).

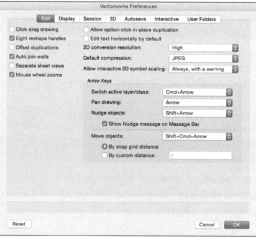

Now when I duplicate the curve it will be in exactly the same position. All I need to do is change the Z value.

Go back to the Design Layer and make sure the curve is selected and choose Edit > Duplicate.

It may appear that nothing has happened but you should now have 2 curves, the new one selected.

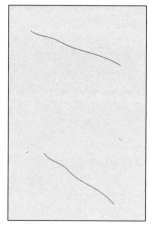

Change the Z value in the Object Info Palette to 3000mm.

This should place one curve 3m above the other, which is at ground level (Z 0mm).

Go to an Isometric view and this should be obvious (remember to switch back on Offset Duplications if desired).

The last step is to create the fabric of the soft surface using the "Loft Surface" Tool.

Choose "Loft Surface" from the 3D Tool Palette.

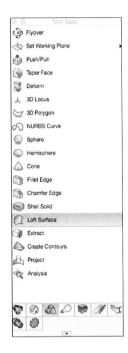

And the first option in the toolbar "No Rail Mode". Click the left hand corner of the top rail then the left corner of the bottom rail.

They should glow red and it should look like this (right).

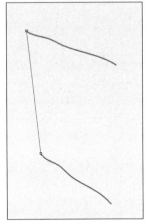

The vertical line between the points is very important. If you click opposite ends the object will try to twist in on itself upon creation and will not work. If it looks like this click Escape and try again.

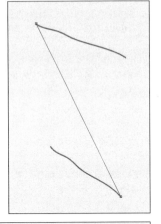

Assuming you object looks the same as the one in the first example i.e with a vertical joining rail then click the green tick in the toolbar.

Loft Surface Tool: No Rail Mode. Select the profile curves.

The next window will offer you some choices.

I have chosen create solid and then clicked OK.

I now have a nice gently curved soft drape to place in my 3D model.
This can be manipulated, if required, using the Reshape function as described previously.

One final use of NURBS, which may be of use as you create you entertainment/theatrical designs, is the "Drape Surface" command.

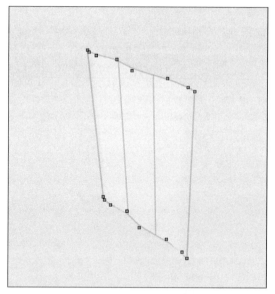

In this example I will create a simple rectangle and "drape" it with a NURBS object.

First I will draw a simple rectangle and extrude it. Approximate size of a long table.

From the Model > 3D Power Pack menue, choose "Create Drape Surface".

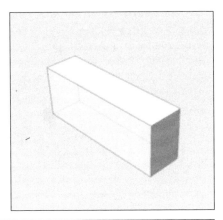

The next window is asking how many U & V vertices will be created. The more you choose the more closely it will follow the lines of the object beneath and the fewer vertices the more unlike the original shape.

I have chosen 20 for each and the Z value of 0, which is the bottom edge of the drape, i.e. the floor. If I wish to stop the drape at 200mm above the floor I would simply enter that value here.

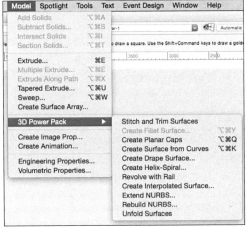

I then click OK and I will see my object with a drape over it and all the control points. 20 x 20 as specified.

It's important to remember that this is a new object, the shape beneath remains as it was. I can easily move this drape away and edit it further and/or delete the original box.

The possibilities for 3D work in Vectorworks are endless. The best option is to have a play and see what each tool is capable of.

The creativity is in your hands.

4 SHEET LAYERS AND VIEWPORTS

In this chapter we will look at how to represent our 3D model on a 2D sheet of paper or scaled .pdf file. We will do this by creating a basic 3D model of a set of three treads in the Design Layer, Looking at it from various angles, such as top, front and sides through "Viewports" and sending those views to a virtual piece of paper, "The Sheet Layer".

The Sheet Layer will have a defined size, such as A3, and the Viewports will be scaled appropriately to fit on this piece of paper. Our model, in the Design Layer, will remain at a 1:1 scale.

Layers

When I open a new document a single new Design Layer will be set up by default "Design Layer-1".

In this chapter we will only be using one Design Layer but as your drawings increase in complexity there will be a need to create more layers in order to manage your drawing properly. Although you can use Layers and Classes anyway you like within your drawing, for now, think of Layers as physical "slices" of your drawing with a real position in 3D space. For example, my 3D models of theatres have Layers such as "Pit", "Stage Level" "Flyfloor" "Grid". Each of those have a height (or Z dimension) with the Pit Layer set with a Z height of -3000mm, The Stage Layer a Z height of 0, The Flyfloor Layer a Z height of 7200mm and the Grid Layer a Z height of 15800mm.

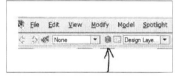

In the previous Chapter we set up and edited Classes in the Organisation Palette. We use the same Palette to set up and edit Layers too – also Viewports and Sheet Layers, which I will explain a little later.

You can access the Organisation Palette > Layers tab

by clicking the icon in the top toolbar that looks like a stack of papers. This normally sits to the right of the Classes icon.

After clicking this Icon you will be presented with the same Organisation Palette we saw in the previous Chapter but this time, the "Layers" tab will be active.

Although we won't be using a Z height in this chapter let's quickly see how it is easily set by clicking on the "edit" tab within the Design Layers window.

There are many options within this window which are primarily used for architectural building use. The values we are normally concerned with are the name of the Layer (It's always good practice to clearly name your layers), the scale (which should be the same throughout your project to avoid getting into confusion) and the Elevation which (as it states) is the "height" above or below "relative to the ground plane".

As stated earlier we will only be working on one Layer for this chapter so it's safe to cancel this screen and return to our Design Layer.

Back to our drawing

Let's draw a set of three treads and extrude it to a 3D object.

Before you start, make sure you have the "Right" view selected as the "current view" (as in the screengrab below) and "orthogonal view" set in the View>Projection menu.. This is critical as we will be drawing the right side of the treads.

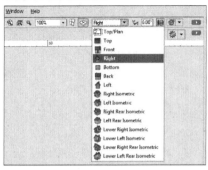

Next, choose the PolyLine tool > Corner Vertex Mode.

Click once in the centre of the page and draw a line vertically. Type 600 into the floating toolbar, hit return to confirm and return again to set the line. Then move your mouse left and type 200 into the floating toolbar and return, return. Next is down 200, return,

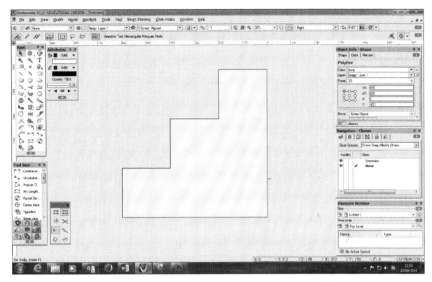

return and so on to create the right side elevation of the three treads. When you have finished the three treads connect the line back to your starting point to complete the polygon.

It should look like the drawing above.

We now want to make this basic object 3D.

Select the shape and go to Model > Extrude.

You will see a box appear asking for the extrusion dimension. Type 1200 into this box to extrude our shape towards us by 1200mm. We are now looking, side on, at a 1200mm wide three tread with 200mm treads and risers.

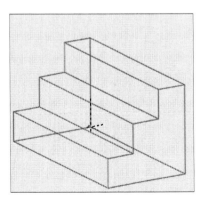

Just to confirm click the Flyover tool, Object Centre Mode and have a look at your three treads.

When you have settled on a nice 3D view have a look in the Object Info Palette.

You will see that the object is an extrude, is on

Layer "Design Layer-1" but has a class of "none". Use the technique learned in the previous chapter to create a new class called "18mm Ply" and assign it a "woody" colour (don't forget "Use at Creation").

Go to the render menu (the teapot icon) and choose OpenGL to see a quick render.

You should see your three tread take on the characteristics as defined by the 18mmPly Class.

We are now finished with our 3D modelling.

Sheet Layers

Think of sheet layers as the piece of paper that you will present your drawing on. Most of the queries I get regarding printing or scaling problems come from people trying to print directly from the workspace where they have just drawn their object.

Think of the workspace where we have just drawn our treads as a 3D space for modelling and now we need to create a virtual piece of paper upon which we will present different scaled views. This virtual piece of paper is the "Sheet Layer".

The next steps will involve "looking" at our 3D model from different angles and creating "Viewports". These snapshots will then be sent to a Sheet Layer of our choice and arranged on the page for annotation and finally, distribution.

Our first decision is what size of paper we would like to present our drawing on. Obviously scale will play a big part in this decision. Our treads will comfortably fit on a piece of A3 at 1:25 but would be too big to represent at 1:10. Luckily we can change all these parameters easily within Vectorworks so any decision at this point isn't set in stone. For this exercise we will be assembling our viewports on an A3 Sheet Layer.

First, let's create our A3 Sheet Layer

Click on the layers icon in the top toolbar as we did earlier, then select the "Sheet Layers" tab within the Organisation Window.

Select New, Leave the Sheet Number as "Sht-1" but name the Sheet Layer "A3".

Make sure "Edit Properties After Creation" is ticked.

Click OK.

Normally, you won't need to change any of the data on this page so you can simply click the "Page Setup" button, which will allow us to set the page size.

In this page we have the option to set the page size based upon common US and UK sizing or create our own.

A word of caution however.

Not all printers print to the same extremes of the paper size and therefore have variances.

If you are using a printer which is attached or available to your computer i.e. the computer can select it from the dropdown list available in "Printer Setup", then leave the "Printable Area" set to "One Printer Page". If you select, for example, A3 in the printable area and A3 from your printer it can cause issues of blank sheets printing unnecessarily.

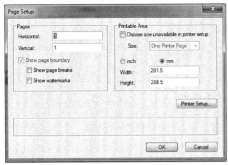

If you are creating a Sheet Layer with a size beyond your printer's capability in order to create a scaled .pdf then tick the button "chose size unavailable in printer setup" and choose the page size from the dropdown menu beside it.

For this tutorial I'll leave the printable area set to "One Printer Page" and choose A3 Landscape as my paper size and orientation from within the Printer Setup.

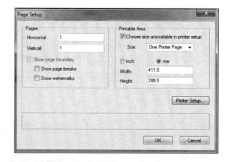

Once you have those options selected click OK.

You will go back to the Page Setup where you can confirm your page size where you can again click OK.

Then you will return to your Edit Sheet Layers page where you can confirm your settings by clicking OK.

And lastly your organisational window will appear, showing the Sheet Layer tab and your newly created Sheet Layer.

Click OK to return to the Sheet Layer in your project.

DON'T PANIC!

It will appear that your lovingly crafted 3D model of the treads has vanished. It hasn't.

What we are viewing now is the newly created blank Sheet Layer which is waiting for us to populate with Viewports.

It the top toolbar you will see that you are viewing Sheet Layer "Sht-1(A3)".

To get back to our Design Layer click the dropdown menu and you will see that "Design Layer 1" is available and by selecting that you will return to your 3D model.

Within our project we now have one Design Layer, one Sheet Layer and we will soon be adding in six Viewports.

Before we look at Viewports let's make our Sheet Layer a bit more attractive by adding in a border and title block. We could do this afterwards, as there's no set sequence, but I prefer to set this up before adding Viewports.

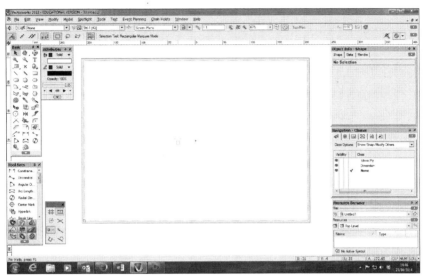

Go back to the Sheet Layer again by selecting "Sht-1(A3)" from the Layers Dropdown menu and you will see the blank A3 landscape page again.

Make sure the Dims/Notes Toolbox is selected in the Tool Sets Palette and scroll down till you find "Sheet Border".

Select it.

Your cursor will now be a large sheet border. You now need to click once on the page, to roughly place the border then click OK to accept the Default Preferences. The default settings for this tool is "lock to page centre" and "fit to page" so there is no need for accurate placement or accurate

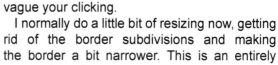

rotation, it will fit itself accurately no matter how vague your clicking.

I normally do a little bit of resizing now, getting rid of the border subdivisions and making the border a bit narrower. This is an entirely personal preference and so you should find settings which work for you.

You can alter the Border settings by selecting the border then clicking Border Settings in the Object Information Palette.

This brings up an edit window.

My normal settings for A3 are shown in the screengrab left. I normally change the margins to 5mm and get rid of the vertical and horizontal zones by placing 0 as those values.

Click OK after inputting your own settings or copying mine.

If I then go back to the Object Information Palette (and assuming the border is still selected) I can see a button marked "Title Block" below the "Border Settings" button we have just used.

Click "Title Block" and you will be presented with this window.

Vectorworks provides a number of default title blocks for you to use or you can make your own. I will cover this in a later chapter but for now, just click the dropdown arrow to the right of the picture showing "none" and select "Simple Title Block-1".

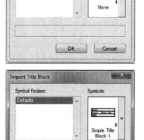

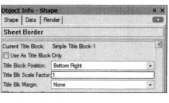

Click OK and you should be able to leave it "as is". However if you want to change its position, size or margins there are options within the Object Information Palette.

Your Sheet Layer should now look like the following drawing.

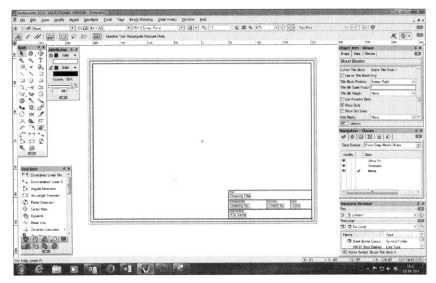

Now let's define our first Viewport and send it to the Sheet Layer

There are a couple of way of doing this, as with many things in Vectorworks, so I will try to use a couple of methods as we build our Sheet Layer.

Firstly, let's go back to the Design Layer and change the view of our 3D treads to "Top/Plan".

Since this is the only object within our Design Layer and we want to send this view to the Sheet Layer we can simply go to the View Menu and click View > Create Viewport.

A Dialogue appears which has a number of options and we must make a number of changes.

Firstly, give this viewport a meaningful name i.e "Top/Plan".

Drawing Title "3d Treads".

Check that we will be sending the Viewport to the Sheet Layer we have just created. (It should already be selected as it's the only Sheet Layer available in our

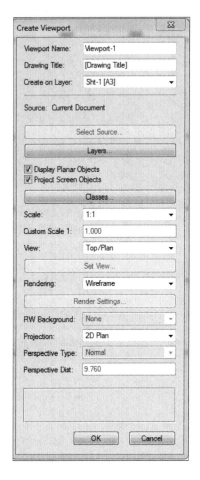
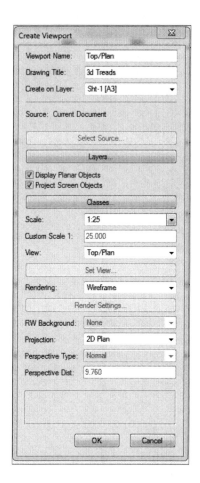

drawing) "Create on Layer Sht-1 [A3]".

And VERY IMPORTANTLY select a scale for our Viewport. I have chosen "Scale 1:25"

Before we move on, note the Layers and Classes buttons. When we get to more complex drawings we can use these buttons and menus to define what Layers and Classes are visible in the Viewport. Just leave them untouched for now.

Reading down the Create Viewport preferences box we can now see that we are sending a top/plan to the Sheet Layer as a 1:25 Viewport.

Leave Rendering set to "Wireframe" and Projection set to "2D Plan" for now.

Click OK.

Your Vectorworks working space will now change to become the Active Sheet Layer, which is the A3 piece of paper, with title block and border and a 1:25 Plan View of our treads.

This "view" can be moved around the page using the select tool, so place your treads somewhere top centre.

The Top Plan View of our 3D treads is now represented on the Sheet Layer.

We now need to go back to our 3D workspace (the Design Layer), change the view and repeat the process again.

We can get back to our Design Layer by clicking the dropdown arrow next to "Sht-1(A3)" in the top tool bar. This shows us the available Sheet Layers and Design Layers in our drawing.

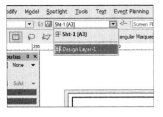

Select Design Layer-1 and you will jump back to your 3D treads.

You may need to Zoom out when you get back to your design layer to see your model again.

Change your view to "right" and repeat the process sending a 1:25 viewport to the same [A3] sheet layer.

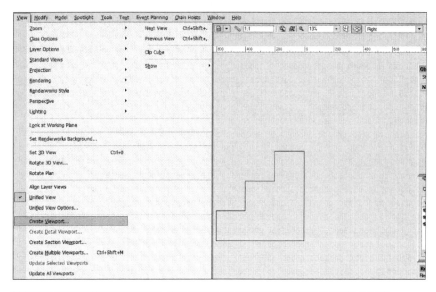

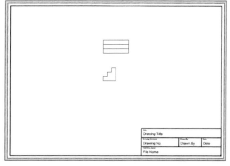

Most of the time you will only need to name the Viewport, select the sheet layer and scale. Projection will automatically change to "Orthogonal" which just means representing a 3D object in two dimensions using parallel lines (not perspective).

Repeat this process another two times creating a left and front Viewports.

Rearrange them neatly as in the picture below.

This arrangement is known as Third Angle Projection. You can do a quick online search

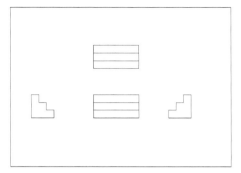

and find out more about this at your leisure.

Just for fun and to practice further, let's add in a rendered right isometric view to illustrate our 3D treads.

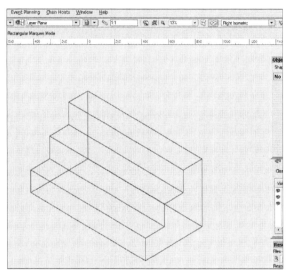

Go back to your Design Layer and choose Right Isometric View.

Repeat the same sequence as before.

View > Create Viewport **BUT,** this time, choose "Open

GL" in the rendering dropdown list.

When you click OK, a 3D representation will appear on your Sheet Layer with a Red striped border.

This is because the Viewport hasn't been rendered yet.

Vectorworks does this to allow you to arrange and set your Sheet Layer up quickly without rendering and re-rendering every time you make changes. If you want to see your Isometric Viewport Rendered make sure it is selected then look in the Object Info Palette. There will

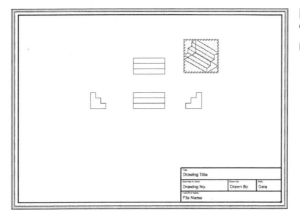

be a button called "Update". This will render your Viewport.

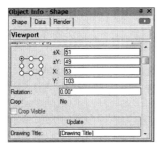

Scroll down the information for the Viewport and note that every aspect of the Viewport is still editable: its scale, the view itself, the layers and classes and rendering to name a few. I'm sure you can see how you could complete the previous exercise in fewer steps by duplicating Viewports and editing their characteristics on the Sheet Layer without needing to jump back and forward to the Design Layer.

You can also find a button in the View menu which will update the selected Viewport or All Viewports if you have multiple Viewports needing rendering.

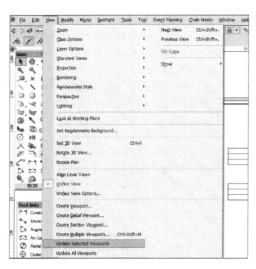

Note that any changes made to the Viewport – scale, classes, layers – will require an Update. In short, if any Viewport has the red striped outline, it needs updating.

Update your Isometric Viewport and you should see the red striped border disappear and the treads will appear with the colour of the 18mm class that you selected back at the beginning of the chapter.

The next step is to add dimensions to our Sheet Layer. This is done by "Annotating" each Viewport.

As a note, we can define the dimensioning convention used in our drawing by navigating to File > Document Settings > Document Preferences > Dimensions > Dimension Standard.

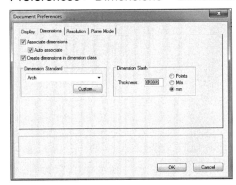

Unless you feel a need to change this, just note the location of the preferences settings for future reference and continue on.

In this section we will be using the "Dims / Notes" Tool Set.

Make sure it is selected. We will be using the first tool in the list "Constrained Linear Dimension".

Select the Plan Viewport then Ctrl Click or Double Click (or Right Click on PC) to bring up a menu and then choose "Edit Annotations". Alternatively go to the Modify Menu > Edit Viewport > Annotations.

Click OK.

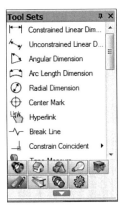

This will bring up a special Orange Bordered Window especially for Annotating the selected Viewport.

Select the 1st tool the Dims/ Notes palette "Constrained Linear Dimension".

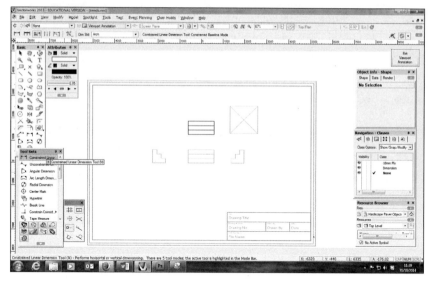

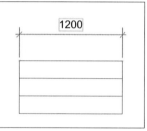

Click once on the top left corner of the Plan View, once again on the top right corner and "pull up" the dimension data to a distance away from the drawing where it can be easily read.

It should look like the drawing left.

Exit the Viewport Annotation by clicking the "Exit Viewport Annotation" button in the top right hand corner. Your Object Info Palette may be covering it so you might need to reposition it a little lower to reveal the exit button.

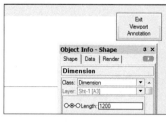

Now let's Annotate the Left Elevation.

Click on the Left Viewport and activate the "Edit Annotations".

Choose the Constrained Linear Dimension again but this time choose the third Sub Option of the Constrained Linear Dimension Tool "Constrained Baseline Mode".

We are going to dimension the risers so click on the Bottom Right Corner of the treads then the top of the first tread and "pull out" the dimension and click to set. Then click the nose of the next tread, and click and then double click the final tread

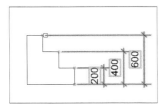

to finish. It should look like the drawing left.

We will now dimension the right elevation treads using a third method just for practice.

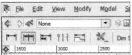

Choose the Constrained Linear Dimension again but this time choose the second sub menu option "Constrained Chain Mode".

Click on the top of the first tread, then horizontally along to where it meets the riser and pull up the dimension to a suitable height. Then click again at the intersection of each tread and riser and finish with a double click at the far right of the last tread. It should look like this. (My font is a little large for the dimensions to sit neatly side by side but this can be easily changed by adjusting the "Text > Size" option from the main toolbar in a similar way to most standard word processing programs.)

Exit the Viewport Annotation back to the Sheet Layer then back to the Design Layer.

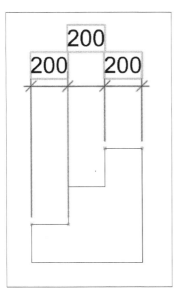

For this final exercise we will add a different scaled, cropped viewport just for practice.

Make sure the Design Layer is Active.

Use the Flyover Tool to position the treads at a Custom Angle (i.e. not one of the standard Isometric).

There's no reason you can't use a standard ISO view. I'm just encouraging you to use different tools and views to become more familiar with the workspace.

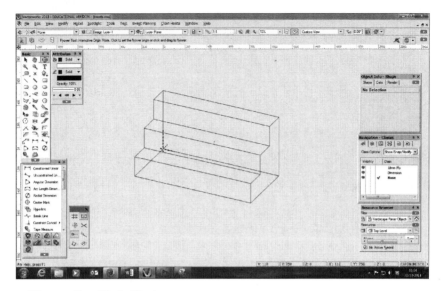

Choose the Circle Tool.

Then change the "Active Plane" in the Top Toolbar to "Screen Plane" rather than "Layer Plane" (you must complete those steps in that order for "Screen Plane" to be available in the Active Plane dropdown list).

The Screen Plane allows us to draw a shape (in this case a Circle) on the same plane as the computer screen, i.e not with any reference to the angle of the treads. If the active Plane remains as Layer Plane, Vectorworks will attempt to align your circle to one of the XYZ planes of the model.

Layer Plane Circle

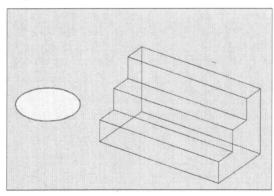

Screen Plane Circle

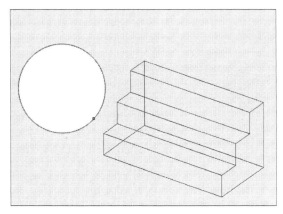

Select the Circle Tool and draw a circle over part of the 3D View.

Make sure the Circle is still the active object then go to View > Create Viewport.

A message will pop up saying "The selected object may be used as the Viewport's Crop". Do you want to use this object as the crop?"

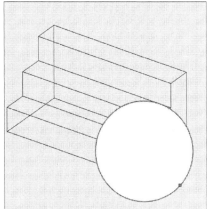

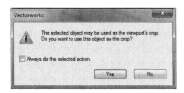

Click YES and we will enter the familiar "Create Viewport" Options Box again.

Name the Viewport "Detail" and again "Create

on Layer [A3]". This time however choose a different scale, 1:10 and choose a different render "Shaded Polygon" and click OK.

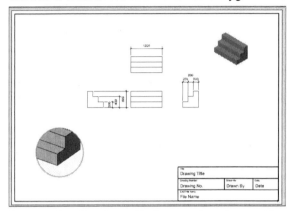

We will pop back to our sheet layer and you will see your 1:10 Cropped Viewport alongside the other viewports. Position it in a corner somewhere and "Update" the Viewport from the Object Information Palette.

Let's add a note on the 1:10 Viewport for the construction team that screw heads must be countersunk and filled.

Click on the new 1:10 viewport and Edit Annotations.

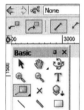

In the basic tool palette choose "Callout Tool".

Choose the second option in the Sub Menu.

Click once within the Viewport (on the top edge of the tread) and once again outside the Viewport to place where you want the text to be displayed. A "Notes Manager Callout Box" will appear where you can type the text which you wish to appear.

Type "Countersink and Fill Screw Heads" and click OK.

Exit the Viewport Annotation.

This is just an example of how you can easily place different views, cropped or full, scaled differently, annotated and rendered onto a single defined sheet layer.

Date and Name your Drawing.

Double Click on the Title Box in the Bottom Right Corner which will launch a new window allowing you to enter the required information as prompted.

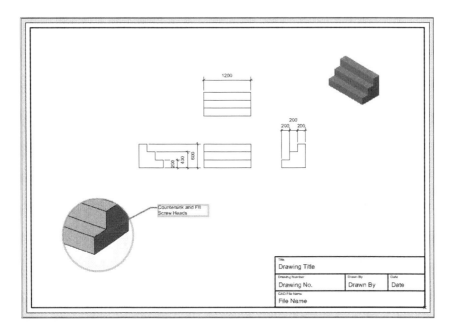

Printing

You can simply print from the Sheet Layer into an A3 piece of paper and the scale will be correct. Make sure "fit to printable area" or similar is NOT selected in your printer's dialogue box.

File > Print Select your printer and A3 paper size and click OK.

Print to PDF

Alternatively you can export to PDF which will create a .pdf document which will be the correct scale.

File > Export > Export PDF.

A dialogue box will appear with lots of options. Most of the time you can just click OK at this point and accept the default settings which outputs your sheet view to a scaled PDF. Give it a name and save it somewhere sensible.

Always put the paper size and scale in the file name i.e. "3Treads1-25@ A3.pdf".

5 DIMENSIONING

Although basic dimensioning was covered in the previous chapter I thought I'd add a little bit more information in this Chapter and cover the most common dimension tools in a little more detail.

At the bottom of the Basic Tool Pallette in the Spotlight Workspace are five dimension tools. These basic annotation tools, and many more, can also be found in the Dims/Notes Toolset.

I will explain these 5 basic annotation tools in a little more detail.

 These five tools are used for adding dimensions to lines, angles, curves and circles.

Linear Dimension places a dimension in either the horizontal or vertical plane.

 There are several options as noted in the screengrab left.

The first option is a simple linear dimension as used the the previous chapter.

I have drawn a 2000mm x 1000mm rectangle.

I then choose the linear dimension tool and the first option, "Constrained Linear Mode".

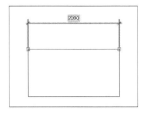 I click once at the start point of my dimension and again at the end point. (In this case the two top corners of the rectangle). I then move the mouse away from the object the required distance I wish my dimension text to appear and click again to place it.

Note that the text size can be altered by ensuring the dimension is selected (as on the left) and then using the Text > Size option from the toolbar.

In this next example I have rotated the rectangle and used the same tool. Note that the dimension is NOT the length of the rectangle side, which we know is 2000mm, but the distance that the angled line takes

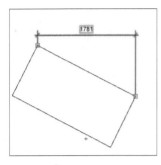

up in the horizontal plane. Be careful of this, it's very easy to get this one wrong in your dimensioning.

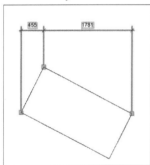

The next option is "Constrained Chain Mode" where a series of dimensions are required. When the option is selected you simply click the first, second, third, fourth point and so on, and double click the end point. All dimensions will be lined up next to each other neatly.

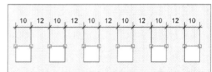

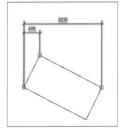

The third Option is the "Constrained Baseline Mode" which is very similar to the constrained chain mode but this time all dimensions are taken from a defined single point (baseline).

This can be very useful for referencing scenic elements from the setting line. Note that in the example on the left I only clicked on each corner then double clicked to end. Vectorworks spaced the dimensions out vertically and evenly spaced.

The next option is "Ordinate Mode".

Use this option to define a series of distances from one fixed point, where you want to see the measurements without dimension lines. You can use the Ordinate Dimension mode to measure either horizontal or vertical distances.

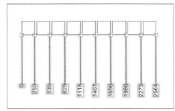

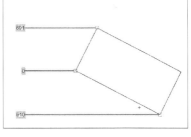

The final Option is "Selected Objects Dimension".

First select an object, then this option. Click once inside the object then again outside the object.

Vectorworks will place a linear dimension of the widest span of the object to the side you clicked.

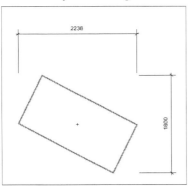

Unconstrained Linear Dimension

The second Tool in the Dimensioning Series allows you to measure the lengths of objects without being constrained by the vertical or horizontal axis.

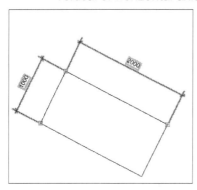

Look back to the first example of the Constrained Linear Dimension tool. I could only measure the horizontal distance of the rotated rectangle side.

This "Unconstrained" tool allows me to measure the length of the side itself even if the shape is not aligned vertical or horizontal.

Not the text is placed parallel to the dimension being measured.

The Chain Dimension & Baseline Options within the Unconstrained Linear Dimension Tool behave in exactly the same was as previously explained in the Linear Dimension Tool.

Note that the way the dimensions are displayed can be changed within the "Dimension Standard" dropdown box beside the tool in the top toolbar.

Or, if the dimension is highlighted, it can be changed in the Object Information Palette.

In the screengrabs above and left I have chosen the ASME standard from the dropdown box.

This has placed arrowheads at the end of the dimension lines.

I tend to use dotted lines and the "Arch" Standard for Dimension Lines but it can be useful to know how to change options as shown in this construction drawing screengrab

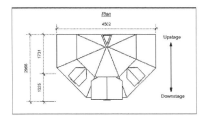

where Upstage & Downstage are indicated by solid lines with the ASME arrowheads.

The next Dimensioning Tools deal with angles.

Angular Dimension measures the angle between two objects, two sides of an object, an object and a reference line or two reference lines.

The first option is simply measuring the angle between two objects. In the example below the object has been selected, then the Angular Dimension Tool, then the next two mouse clicks will define which two lines will make up the angle.

The cursor will point to a pointing hand and the lines of the shape will glow red as the cursor passes over them.

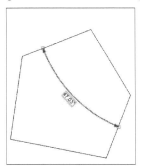
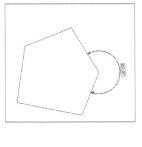

Note that the lines do not have to be connected and dimensions can be interior or exterior.

Precision can be controlled via the Object Info Pallette. (In the examples above the precision is set too high and might be better set to 0 rather than 0.00 i.e. no decimal places).

Angle Between Reference Line & Object.
This option can be used when there isn't an existing line to take an angle from.

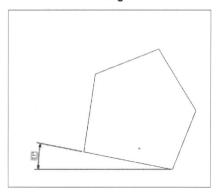

The first and second click defines the reference line, the third click the face which is to be referenced and the fourth click places the dimension text.

The Screengrab left shows the angle between the non existing horizontal axis and the bottom of the polygon.

Note that I have changed the precision of the dimension to "0" in the Object Info Pallette to return a whole number angle rather than the two decimal places in the previous example.

Between Two Reference Lines

This tool can provide an angle between two lines which don't actually exist in the original drawing.

The first and second clicks define the first line, the second and third clicks define the second reference line and the fourth click places the dimension text as in previous examples.

In the screengrab left I have defined the dimension between the horizontal baseline and the top point of the Polygon.

Arc Length Dimension

This tool measures the length of an arc along it's circumference. The options in the Mode Bar allow you to specify how the "witness

lines" are displayed (either in perpendiular to chord or perpendicular to tangent). You also have the option to show or hide the indicator above the dimension text.

In this example I have drawn an arc with a diameter of 3000mm using the Arc Tool.

I have then chosen the two of the arc dimension options to illustrate the difference between perpendiular to chord or perpendicular to tangent

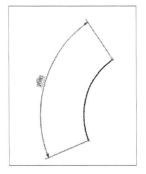 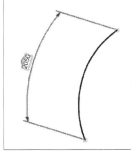

in the screengrabs left.

The Arc Indicator is the little line above the numbers to indicate that the dimension measured is the arc rather than the linear distance between the points.

Radial Dimension Tool

There are four modes and an option to choose left or right hand shoulder mode for displaying the dimensions.

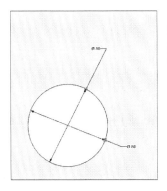

In this example the Diameter of the circle is shown. The top dimension is the left hand shoulder display and the lower dimension is the right hand shoulder mode.

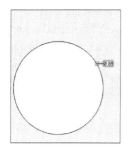

In the example below I have chosen the second mode, which places the diameter information outside the circle.

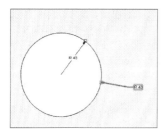

The third and fourth modes show the radius internally or externally displayed.

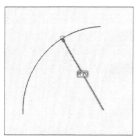

Note that all the radial dimension tools can be used on arcs and well as circles (Internal Radius example left).

Associative Dimensioning

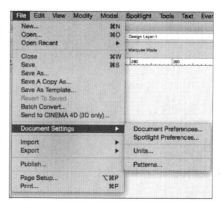

Many of the dimension screengrabs in this chapter show a small green box at point or points that the dimension references.

This is because "Associative Dimensioning" is switched on in the Document Preferences. It should be switched on by default, but if not it can be found by navigating to File > Document Settings > Document Preferences.

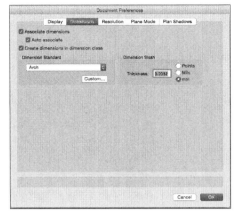

Here you can see that the "Associate Dimensions" and "Auto Associate" are ticked (switched on).

When these options are switched on Vectorworks will automatically link the dimension to the 2D object. Therefore, if the object is edited and changes size, the dimension will also change. Furthermore, we can edit the dimension to resize the object.

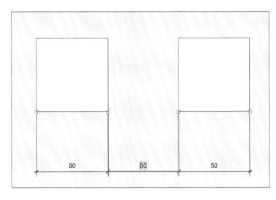

Remember this only happens with 2D objects (and walls) and will not work when annotating viewports.

In this example I have drawn two squares.

You can see that the reference points of the dimension lines have green squares, therefore the dimensions are associated to the objects. I can manipulate the dimension in the Object Info Palette or by double clicking the dimension.

In this example I have double clicked the dimension.

I can now type a new number directly into the dimension box and the objects will move depending on which of the reference points is "pinned". In the screengrab above, the left reference point is pinned and so the right square will move when I type a new value into the dimension field. Essentially I am resizing the gap.

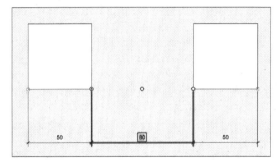

This process can be done exactly the same using the Object Info Palette in the "Length" field and choosing which of the dimension reference points are pinned by clicking the black boxes on the line graphic, exactly as described at the beginning of Chapter 1.

6 VECTORWORKS SPOTLIGHT

In this chapter we will be working in the Vectorworks Spotlight workspace and using a previously created 3D Studio Theatre Groundplan.

Before we start we need to check that we are working in the Vectorworks Spotlight Workspace.

Click on Tool > Workspaces > Spotlight.

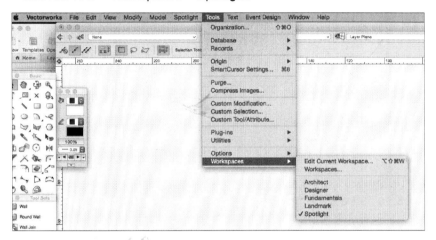

Furthermore, this is the one instance where I would advocate working in scale in the Design Layer. There are various workflows in which this isn't the case but for simplicity, in this case, please change the layer scale to 1:25.

You can do this by clicking the Organisational Palette button (little stack of papers, In the top bar, beside the words "Design Layer 1").

Choose your Design Layer ("Design Layer 1") and Click "Edit".

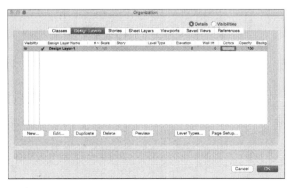

Click "Scale".
Then choose 1:25.

I've also checked the "All Layers" and "Scale Text" buttons.

If you haven't already done so there is a button which is not selected by default but I ask my students to activate as soon as they start using the program. This is a Scale button in the top toolbar.

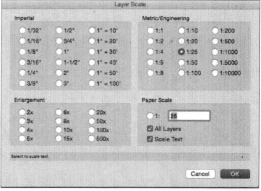

To activate and display the button click the small black triangle button to the far right of the top tool bar.

This will bring up a list of the active buttons on the top toolbar.

You will see there is

a "Layer Scale" button which, by default, isn't activated.

Click this, which will place a small tick next to the words and you will immediately see a small icon with a ruler and the Layer's Scale appear in the centre of your top toolbar. To change scale from now on all you need to do is click this button.

Due to the inclusion of text directly onto the Design Layer, lighting design is the

only time I would recommend working in scale in this way, although there may be many other instances I'm not aware of.

In the remainder of this chapter I will go through the method of placing lighting instruments onto an existing venue plan. I am not a lighting designer and so the chapter should be seen as a guide to using Vectorworks rather than a guide as to how to work on a lighting design.

The venue I am using is a studio venue which I have already modelled in Vectorworks. It has three catwalks and a number of fixed lighting bars as well as some temporary bars which span between the catwalks. It is not critical that you must have a 3D venue; you can still use Vectorworks as a powerful lighting design tool to easily place lighting instruments over a 2D drawing but, obviously, you wont be able to see any of the 3D representations.

After reading other chapters in this book you should be able to create a very basic 3D representation of your space or venue by drawing simple walls or extruding simple shapes.

This is the venue I'll be using. Let's have a quick look around this working drawing so that we can see how the Layers, Classes & Resources are set up within a working Vectorworks model.

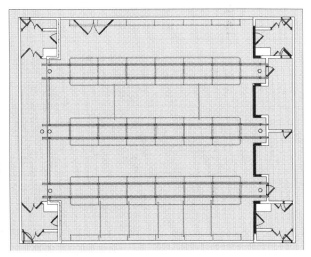

⦿ Details   ○ Visibilities

Classes   Design Layers   Sheet Layers   Viewports   Saved Views   References

Visibility		Design Layer Name	#	Scale	Z	ΔZ	Colors	Opacity	Background
⦿	✔	LX Fixtures	1	1:25	4750	0	▨▨▨	100	
X		Dimmer Outlets	2	1:25	0	0	▨▨▨	100	
⦿		LX Bars	3	1:25	4750	0	▨▨▨	100	
X		Catwalks	4	1:25	4150	0	▨▨▨	100	
X		Tab Track	5	1:25	4000	0	▨▨▨	100	
⦿		Galleries	6	1:25	3600	0	▨▨▨	100	
X		Seating	7	1:25	0	0	▨▨▨	100	
⦿		Walls	8	1:25	0	0	▨▨▨	100	
⦿		Floor	9	1:25	0	0	▨▨▨	100	

Layers have been set up as physical slices of the actual space so each layer has a Z Value which defines its "height" above the ground level of zero. For example, in the screengrab above, the tab track Layer has a Z value of 4000mm and so anything drawn on that layer will be sitting four metres above the floor. It is therefore vitally important to make sure you are drawing or dropping symbols on to the correct layer.

Floor, walls and seating all sit at floor level or Z0.

Galleries have a floor level of 3600mm which is also the floor level of the control boxes.

Tab track is the height of the tab track which circles the space at 4000mm.

The catwalks sit at 4150mm. This is the floor level of the three catwalks which cross the space left to right (550mm higher than the gallery floor).

Lighting fixtures and LX bars are both set at 4750mm which is the height of the lighting bars above the stage floor.

I'm going to place my lighting instrument symbols on Layer "LX Fixtures".

Dimmer outlets don't really need to occupy 3D space (I know they're on the catwalks) so they just exist on a Z layer set to 0. They are placed second in the stacking order (the column left of scale). That mean that when the layer is switched on dimmer outlet numbers it will appear as an overlay so you can assign dimmers to your lighting instruments. Stacking layers can be re-ordered at any time just by clicking and dragging the layers around in this window.

In the screengrab above the LX Fixtures layer is "active" due to the tick next to the words "LX fixtures". Dimmer outlets, catwalks, tab track and seating are all switched off.

Classes in this drawing are mostly the building blocks of the venue. The only class we will be using in this example is "LX Fixtures". Make sure all lighting instruments are placed in a class so that you can control their visibility later.

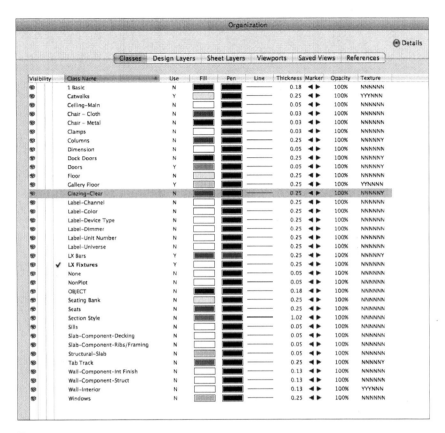

Resources

On the right hand side of your screen is the Resources palette. If you have multiple drawings open you can browse and use resources from any of the open drawings. This is extremely useful but you must pay attention as to which drawing's resources are visible in the palette.

A good tip is to keep an eye on the little red house "home" icon here.

In the screengrab above I am browsing the files within "Untitled 1" and the red house icon is available. If I click the house I will be taken to the files within the open document in the workspace – which is where I want to be. Home.

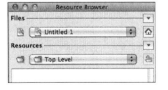

The name in the box has changed to the name of the venue drawing "3D Chandler Update Sept".

If you scroll down and explore the resources within the active drawing you will see a number of folders and textures and symbols. You will eventually find the lighting symbols, which is what we are interested in.

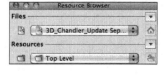

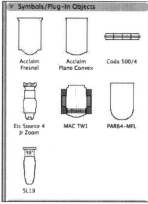

You will notice that specific lighting symbols have already been loaded into this plan. These are the lights which are available as stock in this Vectorworks Venue file.

Placing Lighting Instruments on the Plan

Firstly note that the bars you will hang your lights on are defined as "Lighting Position Obj(ect)". I have numbered these Lx 1 – 8 starting from the furthest FOH bar to the furthest upstage. It is very important for these bars to be defined as Lighting Objects in order for the lights to attach themselves to the bar.

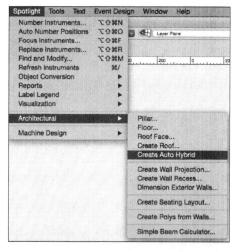

You can make an LX bar by using the Extrude Along Path command as demonstrated in Chapter 3, then create a Hybrid Symbol.

Then Convert the Object to a Lighting Position.

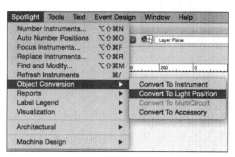

Or, use one of the Lighting Position Tools in the Spotlight Tool Palette such as Truss or the new Lighting Pipe Tool in Vectorworks 2015.

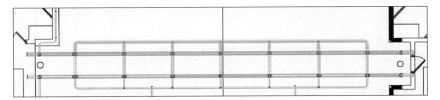

The bar above has been selected and the Object Info Screengrab to the right confirms that it is a Light Position Obj.

The Position Name (Bar Number) is LX7.

Lighting Instruments are generally dropped onto Lighting Objects but you can place lighting objects anywhere in the space. They just might look a bit odd in 3D view floating in mid air. If you want to place lights on the floor remember to change the active layer to "Floor".

In the Navigation Palette, make sure the LX bars, LX fixtures, galleries, walls and floor layers are visible. You can turn the others off.

If I navigate to the Resource Browser I will find the Selecon Acclaim Fresnel lighting symbol.

If you haven't imported any Lighting Object into your own drawing you can do that by clicking on "Add New Favourite Files".

Then navigating to Vectorworks > Libraries > Objects Entertainment and choose any of the manufacturer's symbol libraries.

You should now have Lighting Symbols in your Resource Browser.

DOUBLE CLICK the symbol in the resource browser (don't drag) then click again on LX bar 8, in the centre, pointing downstage as a centre backlight.

The first click will place the lighting instrument, then, as you move the mouse the position of the lantern will rotate. When you have the unit in the correct position click again to place it.

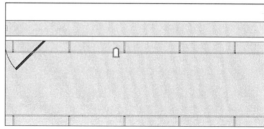

If you have done this correctly the Object Information Palette (assuming the lighting instrument is still selected) will read "Lighting Device".

IF it reads "2D/3D Symbol", something went wrong. Delete the symbol from the plan and try again.

Make sure Layer and Class are set to "LX Fixtures".

The difference between the symbol understanding it's a lighting device and not just another symbol is critical. The Lighting Device has a number of parameters such as colour, beam angle, channels, gobos, etc. A 2D/3D symbol is just a collection of lines and shapes with none of the critically embedded data which we need in order to use Vectorworks as a lighting programme.

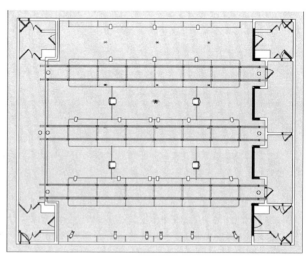

So, we have one Lighting Object hung upstage centre as a backlight. Let's add some more.

I have used a mixture of Acclaim Fresnels and PCs (Plano Convex). ETC Source Four Juniors and a few MAC TW1s to create a basic rig as shown on previous page.

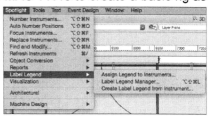

We will now create a Label Legend so that we can show colour, unit number, channel and dimmer information on the instrument symbols on the lighting plan.

Navigate to the Spotlight Menu and select Label Legend > Label Legend Manager.

This will bring up the Label Legend Manager Window.

I now wish to create (Add) a new Label Legend.

There is the facility here to have multiple label legends which can be associated to different lighting symbols. For example you may wish to have a different Label Legend for your intelligent lighting to that of your generic rig.

For the moment we will just create a basic Label Legend for a generic instrument symbol.

Choose "Add".

We will give the Label Legend a name. I'm going to call mine "RCS Default".

The next step is where we will choose which of the available list of attributes we want to be shown on our Label Legend.

Click to the left of the Attribute to place a tick.

For this basic generic lighting unit I have chosen unit number, colour, dimmer and channel.

I can now choose which lighting instrument I wish to use in order to position my attributes within the symbol.

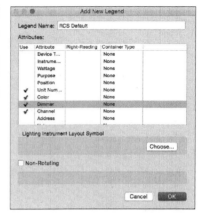

I click "Choose".

Then, I can either choose the symbol assigned or, assuming there are lighting instruments already inserted into the plan, I can choose one of those symbols by clicking on the little arrows to the right of the "Cantat PC" (in the pic above) and navigating to something else.

I chose a ETC Source Four body then click OK and OK again to navigate back to the Label Legend Manager.

You should be back here in the Label Legend Manager with your Legend Name highlighted.

We now need to Edit Layout.

Click the "Edit Layout" button and you will be presented with this, orange bounded, screen.

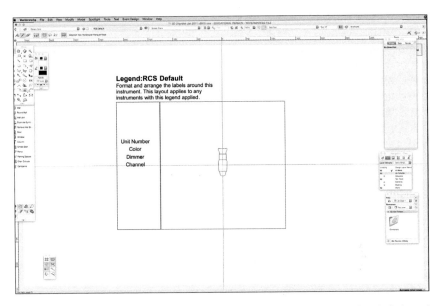

The attributes which we chose earlier are available in the left hand pane and the Source Four body, which I also chose, is centred on the 0,0 mark of the page.

I can now drag the attribute name from the left panel and place it where I want the corresponding information to appear on my plan (apologies if this isn't standard layout, as stated earlier this is just a "how to use Vectorworks, not a how to design lighting").

Once you are happy with this click the big "Exit Symbol" button top right.

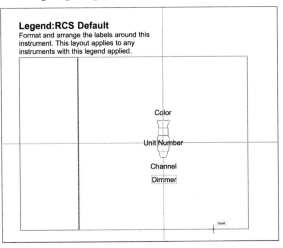

You will be taken back to your LX Plan and don't worry that there is no sign of your beautifully crafted LabelLegend on any of your Lighting Symbols.

Before moving on I have created a second Label Legend

called "RCS Movers" with the following layout using the attributes "User Field 1" (where I can place any information I like), "Unit Number", "Channel", "Dimmer" and "Universe".

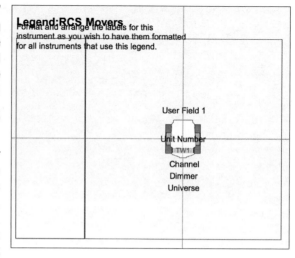

For either of our Label Legends to display the attributes such as unit number, colour, dimmer, channel, etc. then that information must be present in the Lighting Instrument symbol.

We can add the information to our lighting instruments in one of two ways. We can either select our Lighting Instrument then add the information directly into the Object Info Pallette.

OR, we can double click the lighting instrument and add the information into a new pop up window.

Personally, I find this option easier to fill in the bulk of the initial information and then, if required, I can quickly update or change anything in the Object Info palette.

As you can see there is currently no information in the critical, colour, unit number, channel and dimmer boxes. Therefore

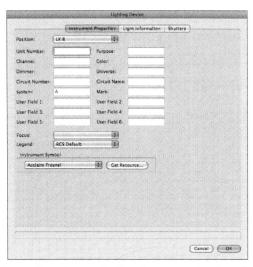

our Label Legend has no information to read. Don't worry about unit number (since we will do that on the next page).

Add in Channel 23 (for the moment).

Dimmer 54 (as defined by the venue dimmer plan).

Purpose "CS Backlight" (helps to define this even though the info won't appear on the legend) and Colour L105. (Lee).

Vectorworks understands and will reproduce light colour by a number of manufacturers including Lee, Rosco, Gam, Apollo and Goboman.By using a specific prefix before the gel colour, Vectorworks will be able to assign your chosen gel to a unit and represent that in a 3D render if desired.

A list of gels and prefixes can be found by searching for "Lighting Instrument Color" in the Vectorworks Help Menu.You can multiple select Lighting Instruments and add information to the Object Info Palette but some lighting instruments will need to be individually selected. For example, dimmer numbers will need to be added individually depending on where the instrument is rigged, but gel colours may be assigned to a group of lighting instruments.

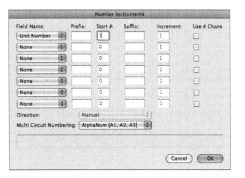

Vectorworks has a tool to make numbering your instruments quick and easy. Unsurprisingly it's called "Number Instruments" and can be found in the Spotlight Menu from the top menu.

You can see that we can select a number of "Fields" from the left dropdown list, assign a prefix, define which number to start from, add a suffix, decide at which increments we will count in and also allow Vectorworks to assign automatically the number of channels that a lighting device requires (i.e 16 for a TW1).

Below the user fields you will see that we can either manually assign the numbers to the lighting instruments (by clicking on the symbols) or automatically from top to bottom, left to right or vice versa.

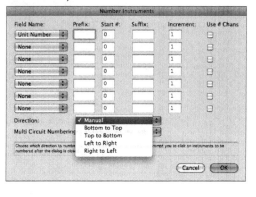

It's up to you and your particular project how much of this information you can assign here in this tool.

At the moment, for simplicity, and since it's only a small rig, let's just number the units and add the other information individually.

In the top field name, click the drop down arrow and select "Unit Number". Leave Prefix & Suffix black, type "1" in the "start#" box so that we will start our numbering at 1 and leave "increment" set to 1 which means we will just count up in units of 1 and don't select the "Use # chans" box since we won't be numbering the Moving Lights in this batch.

Select "Manual" from the direction dropdown box and leave multi circuit numbering set at AlphaNum (A1, A2,A3).

When you click OK a dialogue box MAY appear saying "Select Objects" in the order you wish to number them. Click in empty space to end numbering.

Now click once in the centre of each light, not the movers, from bottom left to top right to assign Unit numbers (1 to 24 on my plan). The lighting instrument will glow red as you move the cursor over it to indicate it is "live" as you click to confirm. Be careful of this, if you are not accurate with your mouse and cursor skills and click without the symbol being red. Vectorworks will assume you have clicked on empty space and finish numbering.

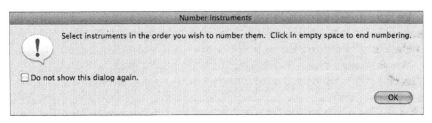

Number Instruments

! Select instruments in the order you wish to number them. Click in empty space to end numbering.

☐ Do not show this dialog again.

OK

You can easily pick up again by double clicking and checking the last lighting instrument you successfully numbered then starting the "number instruments" sequence again but from the next number rather than 1.

When you have numbered your rig (not the movers) then do the same "Number Instruments" sequence again with the TW1s ("movers") but assign them unit numbers 101 – 104.

Now go through your rig and assign.

Dimmer Numbers as per your venue.

Colour from your creative design expertise.

Channel as you see fit.

Purpose Just a basic note i.e. "Centre Backlight" or "General Front Wash".

Now that each lighting unit has the information assigned to it that our label legend manager has been set up to display. We can switch it on by selecting all the generic units (not movers) then going to the menu.

Spotlight > Label Legend > Assign Legend to Insts.

Vectorworks will then ask which of the two Label Legends you wish to assign to your selected instruments. In this case, since I have selected all the generic non-moving units, I can assign the "RCS Default" legend to the instruments.

I'll do the same with the TW1 moving lights and assign the "RCS Movers" Legend to them.

My plan now looks like the one shown overleaf.

If a 2D plan representation is all you need for your project you only really have a couple more steps: one to provide a key to your instrumentation and one to create a sheet layer for printing.

To create your key simply Run the Spotlight > Reports > Key to Instrumentation macro. If you are using Vectorworks 2015, this tool has moved to the Spotlight Tool Set and is called "Instrument Summary Tool".

Remember that you will need to use the "Refresh" button in the Object Info Palette to update the information if you change your plan after running this tool.

Leave all the options ticked and click OK.

Vectorworks will now ask you where you wish your key to be inserted so click somewhere outside the plan. Possibly lower right hand side.

Click and Vectorworks will now place a legend on your plan with lantern symbols, the number of units and number you have used in your plan. If you find you have negative numbers at the end you need to go back and have a bit of a re-design or the inventory data hasn't been embedded

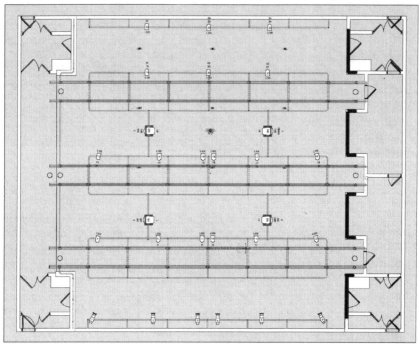

into the plan. Don't worry, it's quite easy to input and something useful to know for other venues.

To update the Inventory stock go to Spotlight > Report> Generate Paperwork.

Click Setup to the right of

Inventory and you will see this box listing the lighting instruments you have used n your design.

Simply add the "number in inventory" into the box. Click on the next lantern in the Inventory Items list and repeat. When finished click OK.

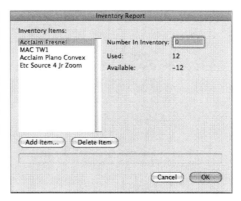

Now, when you click "Key to Instrumentation" you will have an accurate account of the inventory and the units remaining (if any).

The screengrab above shows a symbol of the units used, the amount available in the Inventory of the venue, The number of those units I have used and the remaining units.

For the next step I will assume you read the previous chapter and have a working understanding of Viewports and Sheet Layers.

Make sure your lighting plan looks the way you wish to present it, then click View > Create Viewport and send it to the Sheet Layer required.

Take time to create a Sheet Border and Title Block with, at least, your contact information, the scale and the date.

You can then either print or Export the Sheet Layer as a scaled PDF.

If printing a scaled plan is all you need to do then you can skip the rest of the chapter.

If you are intending on providing a 3D CAD model of your design or create rendered scenes you will need to input some more information as follows.

Firstly you will need to give each lighting instrument a focus point (if you don't its default position is pointing straight down at the floor from its hanging point).

As an exercise, and to aid clarity I have created new Design Layer called "Focus Zones" and split the acting area into a 3 x 3 grid. I will then

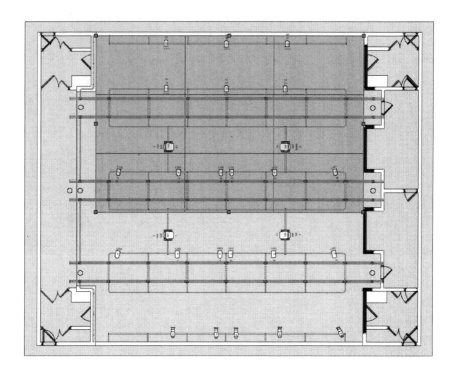

place "focus points" in the centre of each area to assist me with focusing the generic rig.

The areas are marked in the format DSL for Downstage Left and USC for Upstage Centre, etc.

This is useful for assigning your "General Wash" focus points but obviously you will need to add more focus points for specials for any area in addition to the nine generic points.

To add a new focus point select the Focus Point Tool in the Spotlight Tool Set.

Simply Click an area of your plan where you would like to insert a focus point.

A box will then appear asking you to Name the Focus point and give it a height. The default seems to be 1500mm which I think is a little low. You can leave it or change it to 1700.

I have repeated this process and created nine Focus Points at the centre of each acting area and named them in the convention above, i.e. DSR, USC, etc.

The format Vectorworks uses is to select a lighting instrument, assign it to a focus point then turn it on or make it live.

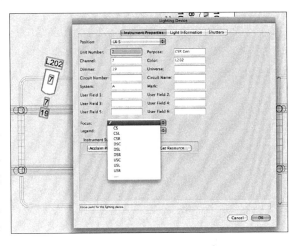

So, let's select the furthest stage right lantern on Bar 3 (in my case Unit 7, a Fresnel) and double click on the symbol. You will see the familiar "Lighting Device" pop up window where I entered dimmer, channel and colour earlier.

Under the Instrument Properties Tab you should see, near the bottom, a "Focus" data field and a drop down list. This list will contain all the focus points in the drawing. If I add more I must make sure I name them. Think about setting up a naming convention since the list may become very large and finding your specific "Act 2 Rostra special" will be much easier with an intelligent name.

For my Fresnel (Unit 7) I chose the CSR focus point.

If I click the next tab along "Light Information" I can see the information about the wattage of the light, the spread of the beam.

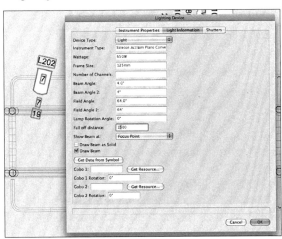

In this box I can see a lot more information about my lighting instrument.

The beam angle and field angle refer to the "focus" or hardness of the beam. Here I can see that beam angle is at its softest with Beam 1 set at 4° and beam

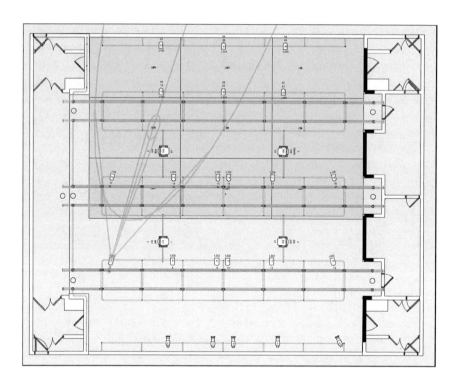

2 at 64° (Ignore Angle 2 for both for the moment.) If I set both theses numbers the same, the beam will have a crisp edge when rendered. If the numbers are far apart it's a soft edge. You can experiment later.

For now I just click the little box marked "Draw Beam" so I can see a representation of my light onstage. Then I click OK.

I can now see a representation of the light beam from the instrument, shown above.

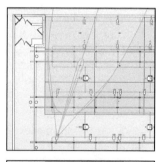

If I double click the lighting instrument again and this time also click the "Draw Beam as Solid" option, the colour of the Gel I have chosen will be represented on the plan.

Here's two examples changing the gel colour to L100 in the first screengrab and L113 in the second.

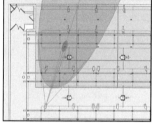

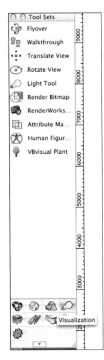

I'm going to add two human figures into the model so that I can light a scene.

Human figures can be found in the Visualisation Toolset (which looks like a lightbulb).

I choose the human figure and (make sure I change the active layer to Floor since I want him to be standing on the floor) and place the figure somewhere onstage.

I'm now going to add in a backlight from USR and give it a blue gel.

*You might need to switch the "draw beam" off to select a lighting instrument within the beam of another lantern.

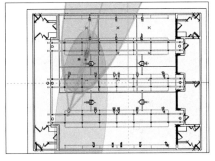

I now have the beginnings of what could (very loosely) be described as a lighting design.

Play around a bit and get used to selecting the instruments, making sure you are on the correct layer, assigning colours and dimmer channels.

Since rendering takes quite a bit of processing power I'd stick to no more than two or three lights as you experiment as you may be rendering and re-rendering quite a few times.

The above plan is quite fun to play with but not a very good representation of what my lights will actually look like. For that I will need to view the stage from the auditorium and render the lighting.

Firstly, I need to go back and switch off any "draw beam" or "draw beam as solid" on lights you will be using (we don't want the orange lines in our realistic render).

I now need to place a virtual camera in the 3D space to look through so that I can see what the audience will see.

The cameras are found in the visualisation palette so I need to open that again and choose the "Renderworks Camera".

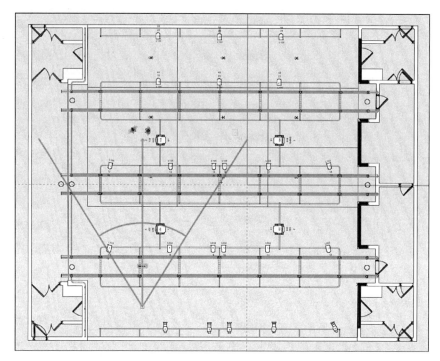

I must make sure the floor layer is active as I will be placing the camera around head height on the floor.

With the camera selected, I click downstage right (where the seating bank would be, between bars 1 and 2) and then click again centre stage right (so the camera is "looking" at the figures I placed).

My plan now looks like the one above.

As the camera is still selected in the screengrab above I can then look in the "Obj Info Pallette". I can see the "Camera Height" and the "Look to height" parameters and adjust them as necessary. Using a little bit of simple maths I can estimate the camera to equal the head height of someone sitting in row three of the seating bank but for now I'll just leave the 1500 defaults.

I'm going to leave all the other selections untouched and click the "Display Camera View" button.

I am now presented with a wireframe view from my camera with your actor(s) standing on stage.

If things don't look quite right I can easily click the button "Top/ Plan View", to go

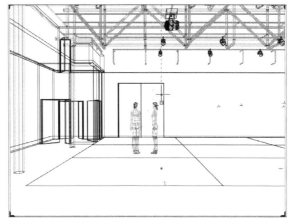

back to the plan and adjust the camera position. If you prefer you can click "Fine Tune Camera View" to move you camera "live" by using the sliders or typing in numeric data. Experiment.

Now let's switch on the lights.

I now need to use a tool palette I haven't used before and therefore may need to go to the Palettes menu and switch it on if it's not already live on the desktop.

Go to Window > Palettes > Visualisation and make sure a tick is next to Visualisation.

There are only two selections to this palette, one with a light bulb and one with a camera.

The light bulb tab lists all the lights on the plan and the camera lists all the cameras (I just set one camera so there should be one there).

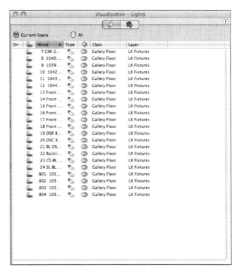

At the moment none of the lights are switched on.

To do this I click to the far left of light name to place a tick in the "on" column.

My two lights were units 7 and 22 . The first number in the name is the channel number followed by anything we wrote in the "purpose" field earlier (that's why it was important) .

I have clicked next to those units to turn them on.

If you are not sure which light is which you can Ctrl Click (RClick for PCs) and a menu will appear.

Click on "Select on Document" will select and move your plan to the light you have highlighted.

Make sure the required light is highlighted, (in my case 22 above) and Ctrl Click (RClick) then select Edit from the menu. Note you can also "Turn On" your light from this menu too.

This will open up a complicated looking window, but don't worry, most of it you shouldn't need to touch.

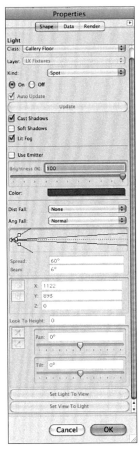

You can see the light is On.

You can select whether the light casts shadows, soft shadows or has the appearance of lighting through fog or haze here.

The colour representation here is the blue as per the Lee 120 that I chose earlier.

Click OK.

If you want to get rid of the automatically assigned complex numbers attached to your lighting instrument names (such as "7 CSR Gen 1041.1.1.0.0.NNA") then you can do so in the data tab box at the top of the same

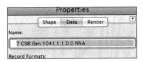

window before clicking OK.

OK, my lights are switched on, our camera is set and my actors are ready.

I have two options here, I can either:

Select the camera again by going to the top plan view and either double click to view the stage from the camera and then use the render menu (teapot) to select Fast Renderworks.

Or select the camera and in the "Obj Info" palette select "Fast RW" from the Render Mode Option and click Display Camera View.

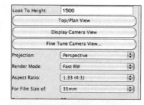

Either way you should see something like this.

OK my lighting design needs some work so I'm going to add in some front light.

I will go back to my plan view. Choose a suitable front light. Assign its focus to CSR. Choose a gel. Then go to the visualisation palette, turn on the light and view the scene through the camera again.

Although my lighting design is unlikely to win any awards,

hopefully the process of placing Lighting instruments, creating Label Legends and generating Inventory Reports in this chapter will help you to use Vectorworks as a powerful lighting design tool.

Production Paperwork

To generate Lighting Production Paperwork navigate to Spotlight > Reports > Generate Paperwork.

This will bring up the Generate Paperwork window.

Click Instrument Schedule then the Setup button below it.

This page allows us to define which fields will be present in our Instrument Schedule and the order of the information. In the screengrab below I have removed a couple of items from the Schedule Columns section by highlighting the words and clicking the <Move button to send the field back to the "Available Fields" list.

I have also re-ordered the Column Order to show Unit Number first by highlighting the words "Unit Number" then the Move Up button.

There is also the option to choose the font, style and size of the column headers and body.

Click OK to return to the Generate Paperwork window.

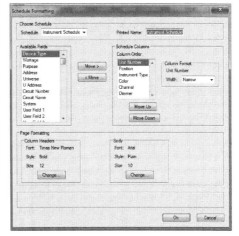

Here I can add in the Header Configuration. I have chosen the order Show, Designer and Date headers then added in the show name, designer and date in the boxes below.

There is also the option to specify the page height and width in millimetres. Click OK.

It may not be immediately obvious but you will now have an "Instrument Schedule" Worksheet in your Resource Browser (along with a new Schedule Format Worksheet).

Navigate to a Sheet Layer then drag your new Instrument Schedule into the sheet Layer.

This creates an Instrument Schedule showing as much, or as little, information as you specified back in the setup pages.

Bear in mind that it is possible to add information to the Worksheet by double clicking and editing the cells but this will not update the information in the actual Lighting Plan.

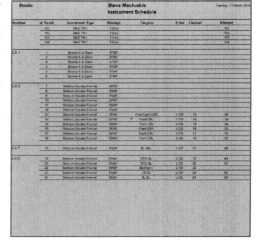

In the Screengrabs right and below right I have added the information "General Wash" to unit 1 on LX bar 1 and the Worksheet now displays that information.

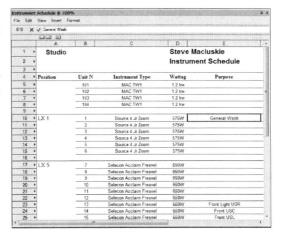

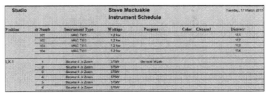

However the information is only present in the worksheet. Lighting Device itself does not show this added information.

A preferred method is to update the Lighting Devices on the plan itself and then re-run the Generate Paperwork command.

I will do this for Unit 2 on LX1.

Select the Unit then Right Click, Ctrl Click then Edit OR Select the Lighting Device and add the info into the Object Information Palette.

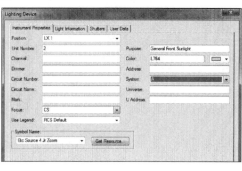

I have added in a purpose "General Front Sunlight", a Colour, and defined the Focus Point.

When I return to my Sheet Layer with my Instrument Schedule it has not updated.

I need to delete the worksheet and then re-run the Spotlight > Reports > Generate Paperwork command again and drag the new, updated inventory onto the sheet layer again.

The Worksheet has been updated with the new information but note that the info I added directly to the worksheet earlier is gone.

With this in mind I would strongly suggest that you ensure that all info is complete on the plan itself, information is added to all Lighting Devices and only when complete, run the Generate Paperwork command.

6.5 VERTICAL LIGHTING BOOMS

Displaying vertical lighting booms on a printed plan *and* being able to show them vertically on 3D renders is a topic of much discussion on many Vectorworks forums and even when explained is still quite a tricky process to understand fully.

Therefore, I've created this small extra chapter to explain, step-by-step, how to use the "Create Plot and Model View" command and illustrate what is happening.

The critical feature of this command, found in the Object Conversion menu of the Spotlight Workspace, is that it will create two new Design Layer Viewports of your booms, one flat 2D and one top 3D. These Viewports will, by the nature of Viewports, display any changes you make to your boom instantly back to the Design Layer Viewports.

To demonstrate what is happening create a 5000mm x 5000mm 'floor' (draw a rectangle then extrude 10mm).

Then we need to create a Boom.

Either do this by extruding an object as below.

Draw a 3000mm line, a 48mm diameter circle then use the Extrude Along Path Tool.

Then create a Hybrid Object by going to Spotlight > Architectural > Create Auto Hybrid.

Then Spotlight > Object Conversion > Convert to Lighting Position.
OR

If you have Vectorworks 2014 or 2015 installed use the Lighting Pipe Tool in the Spotlight Toolset.

Don't forget

Even if you use the Lighting Pipe Tool you will still need to convert the object to a Lighting Position.

Spotlight > Object Conversion > Convert to Light Position.

You will be asked the name the position then be asked if you want to want to make the lighting position a Symbol.

This will be useful if you have many booms the same length as you will be able to re-use your newly created lighting position symbol from the Resource Browser. If your booms will be different lengths then don't create a symbol, just choose "Use Geometry" and create each unique boom individually.

Your object should now read "Lighting Position" in the Object Information Palette.

I would suggest to place your booms somewhere in free space in the Design Layer on the zero line of the Y axis. This will allow accurate measuring and placement of lighting units on the Object Info Palette.

For example the lighting position above is sitting on the Y axis 0 as we can see from the Object Information Palette.

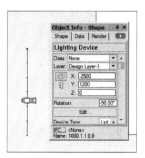

Therefore if I place a lighting unit on this lighting position, its Y position will the distance from 0 or in other words, the distance above the Stage Floor.

In the example above the unit is 1200 up from the Y axis of 0 which, if we stood the boom upright, would be 1200 above the stage floor.

Don't get the Y & Z confused at this point. The boom is lying on the floor and we're only using the Y axis as a way to help us place lights accurately.

Place a couple more lights, select them all and the boom, then run the "Create Plot and Model View" command.

Spotlight > Visualisation > Create Plot and Model View.

Ensure "Vertical" is checked in the next dialogue box then click OK.

Click OK in the next Design Layer window.

Obviously you can rename these later but in the meantime just leave everything "as is" so that the terminology I use will be the same as in your drawing.

Your simple drawing will now look something like thie drawing, right.

The Create Plot and Model View has done three things:

It has moved your original boom drawing to a new Design Layer called "Definition Layer".

It has created a boom Viewport which will be the one you place on your plan to illustrate what will be rigged on the booms.

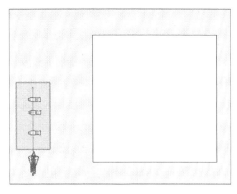

It has created a 3D Top Viewport called "Model Layer" which shows the boom viewed from above and would only be used in 3D visualisations.

To rename, and make sense of your drawing once you get a feel for what is going on I suggest that each Definition Layer is named after the specific boom, e.g. "USR Boom", "MSR Boom" and the Model Layer is named "3D Booms". You can rename these from the Organisation Palette or name them in the step above, after you run the Create Plot & Model View command.

The "3D Booms" or "Model Layer" should be switched off on the Navigation Palette when working in anything other than 3D. I also find it easier to switch off the "Definition Layer" or "Booms" Layer unless I am editing the position of the units.

I can now move my 2D Viewport on the Design Layer to its preferred position for printing, Move the 3D "Model Layer" to its actual position on the groundplan and switch it off. I'll also leave my original "boom" or "Definition Layer" where it is, set to one side, on the zero Y axis.

A final step, to make my drawing a bit neater,

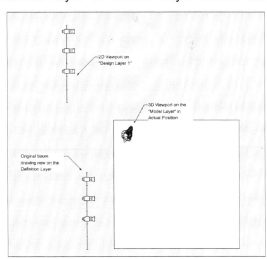

I'm going to add a Boom Base symbol which will sit on the Design Layer and be the 2D representation of the Boom.

I will first create a 600mm square base.

Then, I will <u>drag</u> a lighting symbol from the library, deliberately NOT inserting it as a lighting symbol and place it on the 600mm base. I've used one of the ETC Source Four Body Symbols.

It's very important that this lighting symbol is not imported as a lighting unit as we do not want it to be counted in the final paperwork. Check by clicking on it and the Object Info Palette should read 2D/3D Symbol.

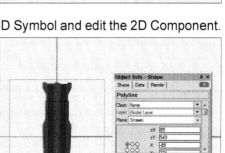

To further clarify on my plan that this is not an actual lighting unit I can double click on the 2D/3D Symbol and edit the 2D Component.

Now I can fill the body of the symbol with a hatch or a block colour to distinguish it from the other lighting units.

I've filled the body with a pattern. It was necessary to fill the body of the unit in two halves, due to the way it was constructed.

Now I can line up my new,

patterned, 2D lighting Symbol with the 600mm base, select both and Modify > Create Symbol.

Once created change its layer to the Design Layer.

Now with the Model & Definition Layers switched off I have a 2D representation of my Boom in place on the stage, a boom detail reference and, if needed, a 3D representation of that boom for renders.

The important thing to remember is that any additions to the booms or moving on units should be done in the individual "Definition Layers" and any changes will be carried through to all of the other views instantly.

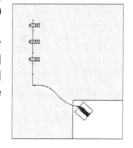

Dimensions can be added to the final Sheet Layer Viewport as annotations.

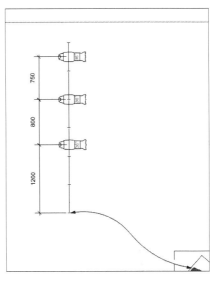

3D View.

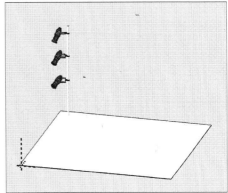

7 CREATING A CUSTOM TITLE BLOCK

First, open a new blank document.

Make sure the scale is 1:1 and set the page size to the size you will be using the title block on. You can scale your title block later but it's much easier to get the scale right from the start.

You can set the page size by going to File > Page Setup.

I've chosen ISO A2 and clicked the "Show Page Boundary" box.

Now I need to draw in the title block using the 2D tools of the Basic Tool Palette.

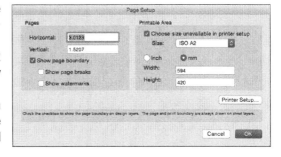

Try to plan this out before you start drawing to make sure you have the right amount of boxes and spaces for logos or disclaimers, etc.

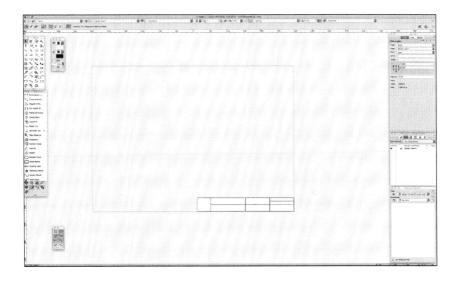

The next step is to add text into the boxes we have just created.

We need to add two sets of text, one which is the title of the box, e.g. "Scale", and a second line of text which will become editable. As we create the text fields it's useful just to duplicate and use the same text although you will probably want to resize the Title Text and the Data Text differently.

I'll start with the Scale box bottom right as an example.

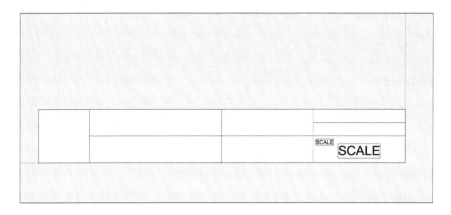

The smaller "'SCALE" text will remain as the title of that box and the larger "SCALE" text will become something like 1:25 when it is edited. The size, position and font will be defined by the decisions you make here when creating the title block so take time to get things lined up and spaced correctly.

Here's my very simple title block.

	PRODUCTION	DRAWN BY	VERSION VERSION
	PRODUCTION	DRAWN BY	DATE DATE
	DESIGNER	CONTACT NUMBER	SCALE
	DESIGNER	CONTACT NUMBER	**SCALE**

I also may want to add an image to my title block; I've left a space on the left.

I can do this by File > Import > Image File then selecting an image.

Remember, for best results, the image should be the same aspect ratio as the box.

I've selected an simple demo image of Saturn but it has been imported far too big.

I can resize this by clicking on the Interactive Scale mode of the Selection Tool and drag the blue handles to shrink the image. If I hold Shift while dragging the handles the image's aspect ratio will remain correct.

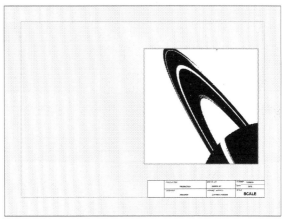

Now that our title block is complete I need to create a new "Record" which is the thing which will allow the title block to be edited using the title block function later on.

To do this I need to create a New Resource > Record Format from within the Resource Browser Window.

Name the Record Format then Click the "New" Button.

The new window now asks us to define a number of Fields, which is essentially our data text "Production", "Drawn By", "Scale", etc.

There are two very important prefixes to these text fields "P_" and "S_".

The P_ is used for "Project" data that is common across multiple sheet layers or S_ which is data which will only be relevant to that particular Sheet. Information like "P_Production Company" will be constant while "S_Sheet Number" will obviously need to change for each Sheet.

Let's add in some text fields. I'm going to use the "S_" prefix for all.

Click New then type "S_Production " in the Name Field and just "Production" in the Default Field.

Create several more text fields, one for each of your title block sections.

After completing this and clicking OK you will see a new Record Format in your Resource Browser Window.

The next step is to create a symbol from your newly drawn Title Block.

Select all the elements of your Title Block then Modify > Create Symbol.

Make sure "Leave Symbol Instance in Place" is checked and click OK.

Now we need to edit the newly created symbol.

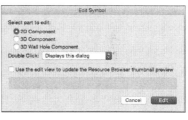

Assuming you have created the symbol correctly, if you double click on your title block now you will launch the Symbol Editor.

Make sure "2D Component" is selected then click Edit.

You will end up in the, orange bordered, Symbol Editor window.

Your symbol will be centred on the 0, 0 X and Y coordinate (centre screen) so the next step is to move your Title Block to line up the bottom right corner with the the 0, 0 point. You need to do this to ensure the Title Block is imported in the correct position when you add it to your Sheet Border.

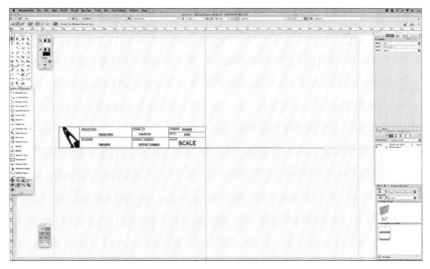

Now select the first piece of text, which will be editable in your final Title Block.

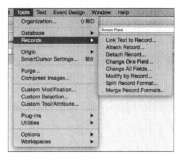

In my example I will click on the word "Production".

Then go to Tools > Records > Link Text to Record.

Then choose which of the Text Fields we created earlier will be associated with this piece of text. In my example "S_Production", then click OK.

Repeat this process assigning each piece of text with the associated Data Fields and then exit the symbol using the Exit Symbol button.

We now need to open the Standard Title Blocks File. (This can be a little tricky to locate.)

On a Mac go to File > Open then navigate to Applications > Vectorworks 2015 > Libraries > Defaults > Sheet Border – Title Blocks > Standard Title Blocks. Then click Open.

On a PC this will be "Programme Files" then the same route.

Now we need to drag out newly created Title Block into this Standard Title Blocks file.

Go to the Resource Browser and make sure the original file is selected, probably called "Untitled 1" unless you called the new file something when we created a new page at the start of this section.

You will be able to see your Title Block and the Record Format in the Resources.

Drag your New Title Block onto the Standard Title Blocks Page.

You may get a window asking which destination folder you want the new Title Block to be added to. If so, make sure you select the "Standard Title Blocks" folder. Then click OK.

Your own Title Block will now be added to the Standard Title Blocks folder.

Now click File > Save and close the Standard Title Blocks file.

To test everything has worked correctly open up a New Blank Document.

Create a Page Size the same as the one you created when designing the new Title Block.

Go to the Dims / Notes Tool Set and choose Sheet Border.

Click on the page to set it. Remember you don't have to be too careful as it will lock, size and centre to the page.

Make sure the Sheet Border is selected then click Title Block in the Object Info Palette.

Click the Icon that says "none" and you should see lots of choices for Title Blocks.

Within them will be your Title Block.
Select it and click OK.

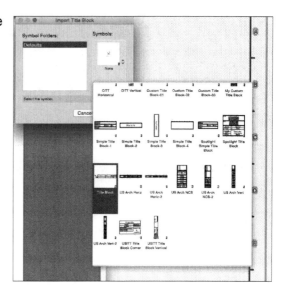

All being well, it will be inserted bottom right of your Sheet Border.

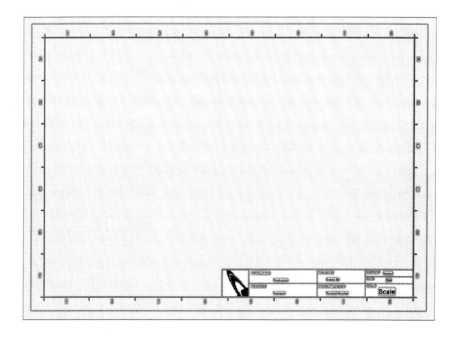

Now you will be able to select "Edit Title Block" from the Object Info Palette.

Then add your own Information into the Data Fields as necessary which will then be displayed in your Title Block on your drawing.

Be aware that all Title Blocks can be scaled using the Title Block Scale Factor. Therefore it shouldn't be necessary to create multiple sizes for your custom title blocks assuming they scale correctly.

I have added Sheet Borders and Title Blocks to Design Layers for the purposes of this tutorial. Please be aware that Sheet Borders and Title Blocks are normally added to Sheet Layers.

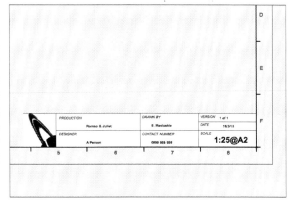

8 SYMBOLS

The use of symbols can greatly speed up your drawing and save you time as well as reducing file size. Any time you have multiple instances of the same object in your drawings, such as chairs in an auditorium or pieces of stage decking, you should be considering using symbols.

There are four types of symbols:

Black – This is the most common type. All the parameters of the object are saved within the symbol definition meaning that any changes to the symbol will change all instances of that symbol throughout your drawing.

Blue – This symbol is essentially a group. When you change any parameters of this symbol definition it is only that specific definition that is changed. The others instances of the blue symbol are not affected. When you create a symbol choose the "convert to group" option.

Red – This is a type of plug-in object such as a door or window. They have specific insertion behaviours and can be modified with many variations of the same object in the drawing. The option to create a red symbol wont be available unless the object is already a plug in object.

Green – These symbols are page based rather than world based meaning they are normally annotation symbols and are scaled relative to the page they are used on.

We will only look at Black and Blue symbols in this chapter.

Let's draw a simple piece of stage decking 2440 x 1220 and extruded to 180.

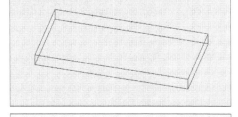

Now, using your 3D modelling skills lets add four scaff legs.

In Top/Plan View, draw one 48mm diameter circle near the corner and extrude it to 1000.

Then Mirror and Duplicate this leg to place the other three.

Select the original extruded rectangle and change the Z value to 1000-180 (This will make the top of the deck 1000). It should look like the screengrab below.

Select the top and all four legs.

Go back to Top/Plan View then navigate to Modify > Create Symbol.

You will then be presented with an Options Dialogue Box.

Firstly, name your symbol.

Next define the "Insertion Point". This

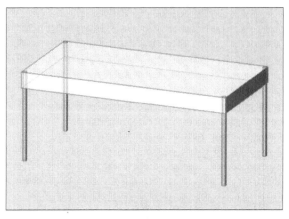

is the reference point which your cursor will place the symbol into a drawing. In the case of a decking unit it will be useful to have one corner as an insertion point rather than the centre of the deck so I have chosen "Next Mouse Click".

World Based units will respond to changes in scale within our Design Layer so make sure that option is checked rather than Page Based.

We don't need the deck to be inserted into walls so can uncheck that option.

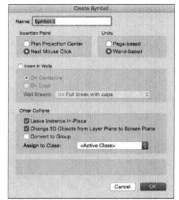

We do want the symbol to be left in place after in converted so keep this checked.

Likewise keep the "Change 2D Objects from Layer Plane to Screen Plane" checked as, If deselected, any 2D planar objects in the layer plane that are part of the symbol will not display in Top/Plan view, so a hybrid symbol may not display properly in Top/Plan view.

And you can either assign the symbol to the active class or manually assign it here.

Now click OK.

Remember we decided to define the Insertion Point by "Next Mouse Click". Therefore, the next screen after clicking OK is Vectorworks waiting for you to define the Insertion Point. Click one of the corners of the deck to define that as the Insertion Point. You will then have a final options box, which is asking you to define the "Destination Folder". This is essentially where you would like this symbol to be created and you will likely only have one option here unless you have multiple projects open.

When you have decided on your destination folder click OK and the symbol will be created.

You should see a new symbol in the resource browser.

If your resource browser doesn't look the same as the screengrab check "View As Thumbnails" is selected by clicking the small black triangle arrow to the right of the word Resources (below the red home/house icon).

Notice the symbol name has a black font. This is known as a Black Symbol.

Our new stage deck symbol can now be dropped into our model space by double clicking the symbol and then clicking on the page.

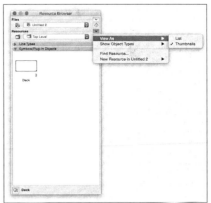

Note the first click defines where the object will be placed, using the insertion point you defined earlier, and the second click defines the rotation.

We can easily and quickly make up some staging now using our newly created symbol.

In order to give the deck some colour I double clicked on one of the decking units, selected "edit 3D component" then selected the top section and chose a colour from the Attributes Palette. You may need to move into an isometric view to select the top of the decking unit.

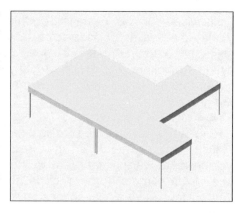

Note that I only need to do this to one of the symbols on the page and ALL the other instances of the symbol changed too. This is the essence of Black Symbols; a change to any of the parameters of the symbol will change all instances on the page.

This doesn't mean that I cant move each instance around, for example raising the downstage

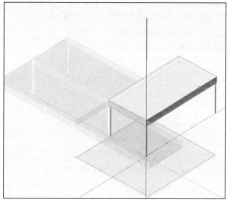

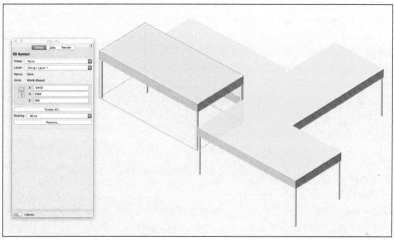

right unit 500mm as in the screengrab below. What I CAN'T do with a black symbol however, is extend the legs of this unit by 500mm without extending ALL the legs of all instances of the symbol.

In order to do that I need to create a Blue Symbol.

Right click on the symbol in the Resource Browser and choose "Edit Symbol" Options. If you have an older version of Vectorworks it's a two step process, "Edit" then "Symbol Options".

Then put a tick in the "Convert To Group" option.

After you press OK you should see that your deck symbol now has a Blue Font. It is now a Blue Symbol.

Now that it is a Blue Symbol I can edit the legs of my downstage right deck unit, to make it more realistic, without affecting the other symbols.

Delete the current downstage right symbol and replace it with the new Blue Symbol.

Double Click on the new unit and the screen will change to an orange-bordered screen. Within this screen you can edit each of the component parts of the symbol.

For ease of selection, change to an isometric view if you are not in one already.

Select the top of the unit and change the Bot Z to +500.

Select the legs of the unit and change extrusion length to 1500.

When you exit the group, using the orange button top right. You will see that only this instance of the deck symbol has 1500mm legs.

This is the essence of the Blue Symbol. I can still use the symbol to create my deck platform quickly but I have the ability to change the parameters of a single instance without affecting the other instances.

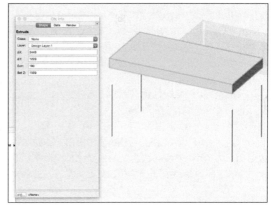

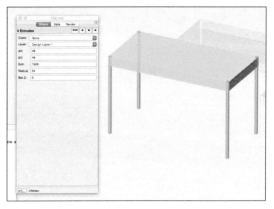

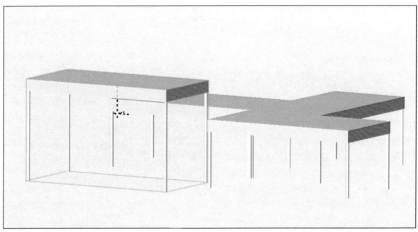

9 SCALING IMPORTED DRAWINGS

In this short chapter I will explain a process I have found extremely useful when importing drawings or plans from external sources.

The "Scale Object" command.

In this example I have received an email with a .pdf attachment for a small staging setup.

I can now see that the designer has drawn up some set elements. It appears to be five pieces of stage decking and three flats.

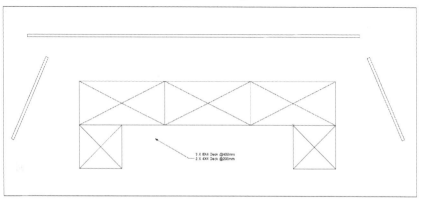

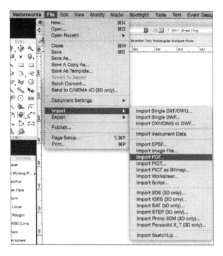

Luckily they have specified the sizes of the deck units and with that information I can re-scale this .pdf in Vectorworks in order to measure the flats and the spacing which has not been provided.

Firstly I go to File> Import and import the PDF.

The .pdf is now imported into Vectorworks.

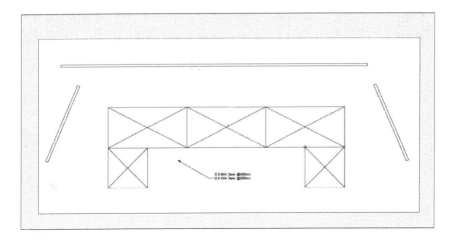

If I tried to take a dimension directly off the imported drawing it would be wildly out. The short side of the 8x4 deck is reading 56mm.

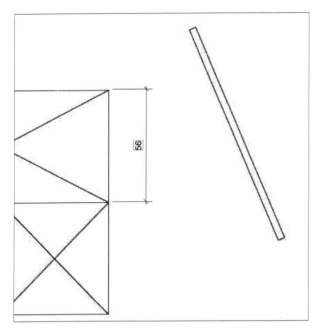

We will not be able to select an individual "object" on the page. Vectorworks just sees this entire page as one picture or object in itself. But we do know the sizes of the elements within the page and so can resize or rescale the entire page.

Choose Modify>Scale Objects and then choose "Symmetric by Distance".

Then click little Icon to the right of the words "Current Distance" and we will return to the .pdf import within Vectorworks.

Now, draw a line along a known dimension. The inclusion of the scale ruler on the page would make this the easiest option (a good reason to include one in every drawing you send out) but in this case we'll draw a line down the long side of one of the 8x4 Steeldecks.

The Scale Objects Dialogue box states that it sees the long edge as 111mm (which is obviously wrong).

We can now type in the "New Distance" in the box provided of 2440mm which, as you know, is the correct distance for the long edge of an 8x4 piece of Deck.

When we click OK, Vectorworks will ask if you want to scale the entire drawing based upon this known measurement. Click Yes.

Click OK and the page will be resized and rescaled correctly.

I can now take other dimensions from the drawing that were not provided in the original .pdf.

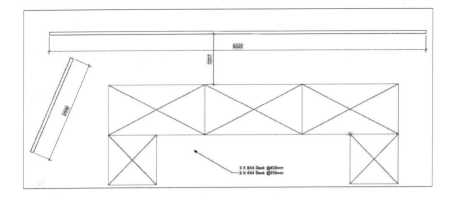

Obviously, these dimensions should only be used as a rough guide and the provision of correctly drawn and dimensioned drawings is preferred. This quick workflow will hopefully allow you to proceed with some work while you wait for updated drawings.

Remember, any known dimension can be used.

10 IMPORTING OTHER DRAWING FILES

In this chapter we will examine how to import a .dwg file and extract individual scaled .pdfs.

Firstly we need to import the .dwg.

This is done by using the File > Import function in Vectorworks.

After clicking the "import single DXF/DWG" option you will see a standard navigation pane where you can locate your .dwg file and then click OPEN.

You will then see this options dialogue box where we will alter a couple of the settings. You can save the settings you make here so that you won't have to alter this options box on future imports.

There are three tabs, Primary Settings, Graphic Attributes & Objects. Vectorworks 2015 has a fourth tab: "Location".

We will look at each tab and make a couple of small changes.

Primary Settings

Make sure "settings" is set to "Active Settings".

The next box "Unit Settings in file" states that Vectorworks has found that the units in the DWG file are millimetres and so the imported drawing will also be in millimetres. You can generally leave this but best to check the "set Vectorworks Units to Match" box.

The model space is very important. Always import at 1:1 so change this from the "fit to page" option and, if you're using an older version of Vectorworks, click "centre after import". Vectorworks 2015 has a new "Location" Tab which allows you to "Centre after Import" this is the default

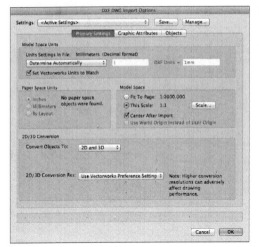

and recommended setting.

Now click the Graphic Attributes Tab.

Graphic Attributes

You can leave most of this page "as is".

Just check the "Add prefix to imported DXF Layers" and write something in the box (I just use "CAD").

This means that the classes which are created by Vectorworks from the DWG / DXF layers will all be marked "CAD-". This allows us to easily separate them from any classes within our own drawing.

Now click the last "Objects" Tab.

Objects

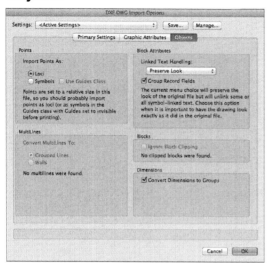

You won't need to change anything in this options box except the Dimensions tick box at the bottom.

Click the "Convert Dimensions to Groups" box. This seems to help retain dimension objects such as arrowheads in the newly created drawing.

Save and call your preset something.

Next time you need to import you will only need to choose your newly saved Settings and all these presets and selections will be automatically loaded.

If you have saved your settings you can click OK to import the DWG.

You may get a message about Font mappings. This is because PCs, MACs, AutoCAD and Vectorworks use different fonts and some aren't compatible.

Just click OK and Vectorworks will replace any incompatible Fonts with its nearest equivalent.

Vectorworks will now import the DWG file. It may take a little while depending on the complexity of the drawing.

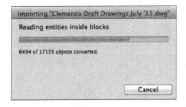

This example has 17, 155 objects to convert.

After import Vectorworks will display the DWG file.

You will see that in my example AutoCAD has all its views on one sheet. I want to create a new sheet layer for each page, essentially as individual viewports on individual sheet layers.

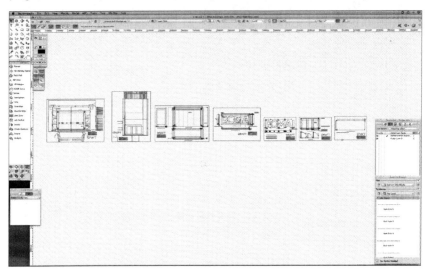

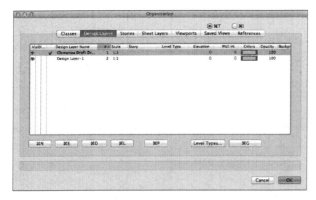

Open the Organisation Palette and choose sheet layers. We will create one A0 sheet and duplicate it a further 6 times to give us the seven sheets, one for each viewport.

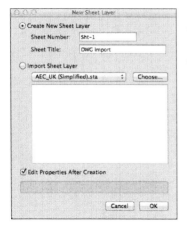

Click the Sheet Layer Tab and New new sheet layer.

Make Sure Edit Properties After Creation is checked, then click OK.

Click Page Setup.

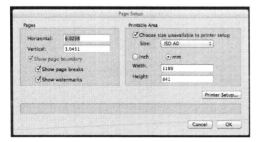

I need to Check the "Choose Size Unavailable in Printer Setup" because I'm only connected to an A4 printer, and then choose the ISO A0 page size.

Click OK on each of the three screens on the previous page to come back out of the setup and back to the Organisation Pallet where there will be a new A0 Sheet Layer.

Now just click the duplicate button to create six more (you can edit the titles of each one by selecting "edit").

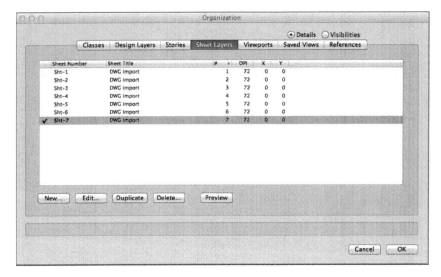

We now have the 7 A0 Sheet Layers ready to send the 7 parts of the DWG plan to as Viewports.

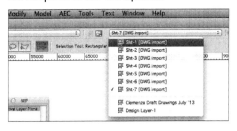

Go back to the Design Layer by clicking the Layers Icon on the top bar and selecting the Name of the Original File or Design Layer-1. Either will work in this instance. (You should also see the seven new sheet layers in this list.)

This should bring us back to the Design Layer with the 7 DWG plans.

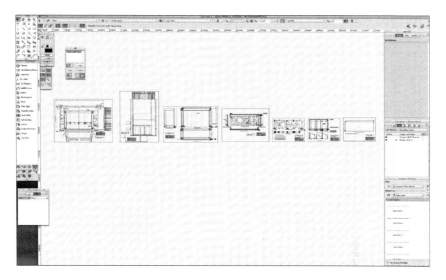

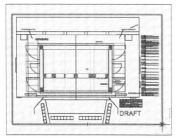

We will now use the rectangle shape to select an area we will then send to the first of the seven new Layers.

Choose the Rectangle Tool and Draw a box around the far left stage plan.

Choose View > Create Viewport.

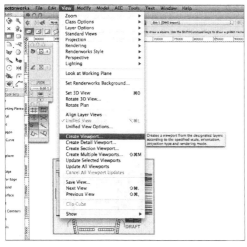

Then Give the Viewport a meaningful name.

Choose one of your previously created sheet layers.

Choose 1:25 scale.

Then click OK.

The screen will change and it will appear that you have lost your work.

This is not the case. It's just that the location of the Viewport you have just created and the Location of the Sheet Layer are a bit lost in space. You can zoom out and locate the Viewport and drag it onto the sheet layer by eye but there is an easier way.

Use the "Fit to Page Area" button on the top toolbar to centralise and view your sheet layer in the screen.

It should snap to something like this.

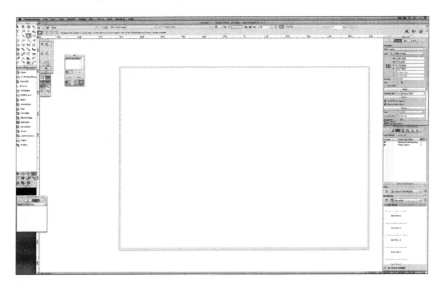

If the page looks different Go to File > Page Setup.

And uncheck the Show Page Breaks and Show Watermarks options.

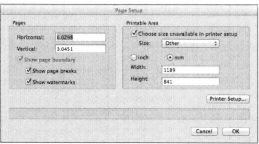

Next we need to place our 1:25 Viewport on the A0 Sheet Layer.

If we look in the Object Info Palette of the Viewport we can see the X&Y coordinates of the Viewport are wildly out.

The easiest way to centralise your Viewport is to simply type 0, 0 into the X&Y boxes.

Also click the central dot of the location icon to ensure the centre of the Viewport will be located at 0,0.

You can either click Enter or Return on your keyboard or Update in the Object Info Palette to bring the Viewport into your Sheet Layer.

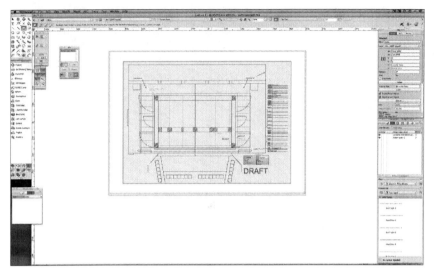

Your Sheet Layer should now look like the drawing above.

You can now go back and repeat the process for each of the different plans.

In Summary

You Create a Viewport by drawing a rectangle round the plan

You send the Viewport to a specific sheet layer

Remembering to give it a name and a scale

You may need to Center the Viewport on that by altering the X and Y coordinates in the Object Info Palette

The Section Viewport will require you to swap around the Page Dimensions to give it a Portrait Aspect.

Creating a Scaled PDF

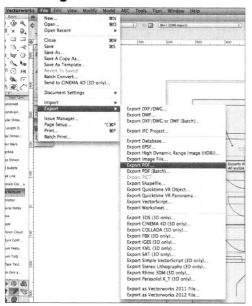

Open any of the Sheet Layers.

Choose File > Export > PDF.

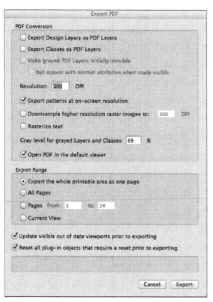

You can leave the next page with the default settings if they look the same as in this screengrab.

Click Export and save your 1:25 scaled PDF.

You may have noticed there is a File > Export > Batch PDF.

This allows you to select multiple Sheet Layers and save them as individual PDF's in one step.

It's quite simple and straightforward so I won't go through it in detail here. Just click the Sheet Layers on the Left and send them to the Export List on the Right.

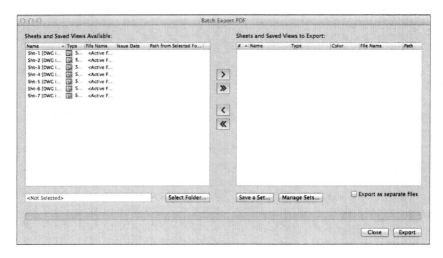

Remember to tick the "`export as separate files".
Export.

11 WORKSHEETS

You can use the Worksheet tool in Vectorworks to count and calculate items in your drawing automatically. This can allow you to provide a key with your drawings showing how many units have been used, how many there are in stock and therefore, how many remain.

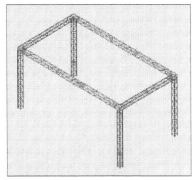

I'll use truss in this example but it can be easily changed to steeldeck, lighting units, sound equipment, etc.

Firstly I'll draw up a simple freestanding truss structure.

Now I want to create a Worksheet that will count the units I've used, compare that to the stock available and show a key on my final layout.

First Create the Worksheet.

Resource Browser > New Resource > Worksheet.

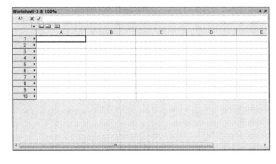

You will be given the option of naming and defining the number of rows and columns (just like Excel).

OK this and you will be presented with a new blank Worksheet.

Type some headers into the top row such as "Truss Type" "Image" "Stock" "Used" "Difference".

(You will need to use the Enter or Return Key to commit the text to the box on the worksheet.)

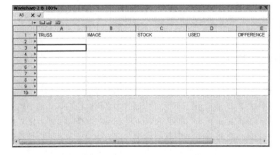

Fill in the data you know at the moment into the required boxes such as the type of truss 1m, 2m, etc and the Stock.

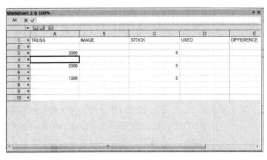

Firstly we'll let the Worksheet count up the number of instances of each symbol for us. We'll start with the 3m sections.

Click on the box D3 (in my example). This is where I want the number of 3m sections used to be displayed.

Then click the small black downward facing triangle here (image left). Vectorworks 2015 has a much simpler Insert > Function menu.

A Dropdown List will appear .

Now select "Paste Function".

This is command allows us to select from a number of pre-defined functions which are available in the Worksheet. The one we are looking for is "Count".

Click OK and this will Paste the Count Function into the Top Bar of our Worksheet.

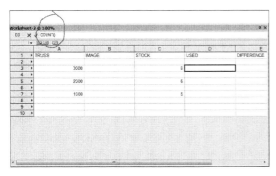

We now need to tell the Worksheet WHAT to count.

Click on the black down facing arrow again but this time choose "Paste Criteria". Again, Vectorworks 2015 now has a simple Insert > Criteria menu.

This screen is a simple series of drop down selection which allow us to define WHAT the count function is counting.

In our example we want the Count function to count objects in the

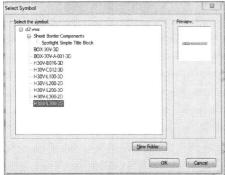

drawing which use H30V 3m symbol.

So, choose the word "symbol" in the first dropdown and then click the small selection box highlighted below. This will bring up a list of symbols in the drawing and you can simply choose the H30V L300-3D symbol.

At this point Vectorworks will tell you how many object meet the Criteria you have specified.

Press OK and this Function and Criteria will be entered into your worksheet.

DON'T PANIC – NOTHING APPEARS TO HAVE HAPPENED

Last step is that you need to

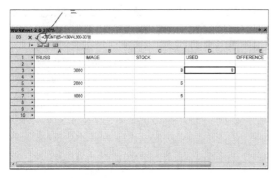

insert an = sign in front of your formula on the worksheet toolbar and then press Return / Enter in order for it to display the result within the worksheet.

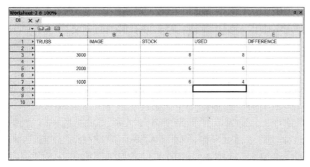

Repeat the process for the 2m and 1m sections.

I now want to add a simple arithmetic function to show me how much stock I have left.

This will be a simple Total Stock Items Units minus Items Used or (in my table) C3-D3, C5-D5 and C7-D7.

There is no need to go back into the Function / Criteria menus, just type the formula directly into the data bar ensuring the correct cell is highlighted.

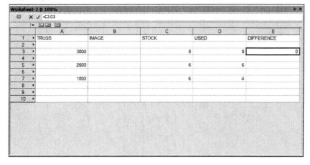

Type =C3-D3 in cell E3 to have "Stock" minus "Used". In this case the result is 0 since we have eight 3m sections and have used eight in our planning.

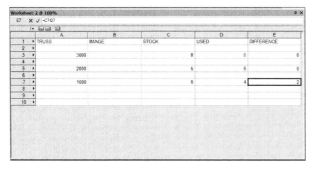

Repeat for the 2m and 1m Truss.

Lastly, I'm going to add a reference symbol into our worksheet.

Select the 3m "Image" Cell (B3) then click on the small black arrow again.

This time select "Image" from the Paste Function Menu.

Click OK, then, Click the black arrow again to select and define the Criteria.

Our definition will be the same as before. Choose the word "symbol" in the first dropdown and then click the small selection box, as before and choose the H30V L300-3D symbol.

We need to add the = sign in again and press enter / return.

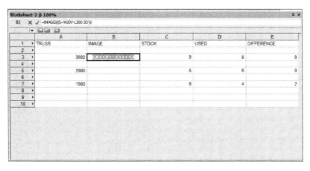

We should now see an example of the H30V L300-3D symbol in our worksheet.

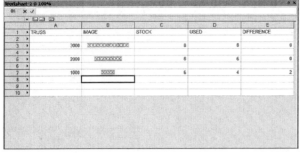

Repeat for the 2m and 1m sections.

We now have a worksheet that we can add to our Sheet Layer which defines the amount of stock we have and the amount used in our design.

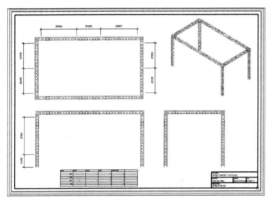

TRUSS	IMAGE	STOCK	USED	DIFFERENCE	
3000		8	8	0	
2000		6	6	0	
1000		6	4	2	

A close up screengrab.

If there are any changes to the design, simply run the worksheet again and the numbers will alter depending on the new configuration.

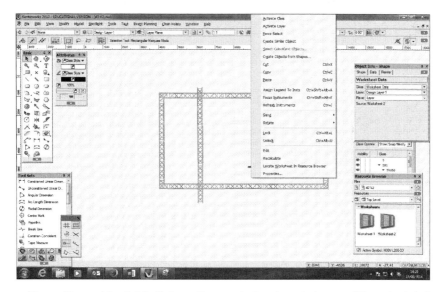

You will need to right click on the worksheet and choose "Recalculate" after any changes.

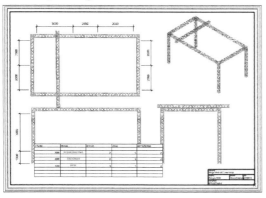

You can see from my quick new design layout that I have used too many 2m sections and that my Worksheet is reading -3.

TRUSS	IMAGE	STOCK	USED	DIFFERENCE
3000	XXXXXXXXXXXXX	8	8	0
2000	XXXXXXXXX	6	9	-3
1000	XXXX	6	4	2

As a final note, you can see that my Worksheet is a little too big for my A3 Sheet Layer when I apply it so I need to do a little bit of formatting to make it fit.

Formatting can be done by right clicking the worksheet and selecting the "edit" option.

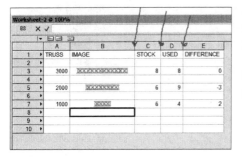

I can then click and drag the column widths to make them narrower.

And I can select and delete the extra rows that I'm not using.

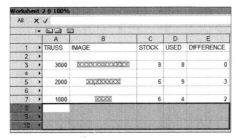

Select the Cells, Right Click > Delete > Rows.

When I have finished editing I can exit from this screen and see my new, efficiently sized Worksheet on my Sheet Layer.

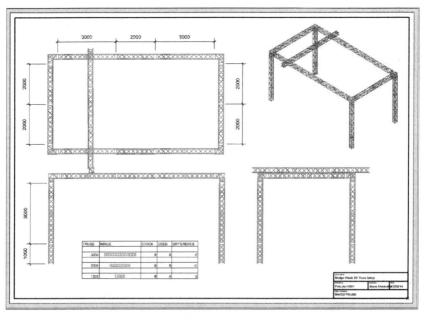

There are plenty of other options within the Worksheet Edit Screen > Format Cells such as Font Size and Type, Alignment, Borders and

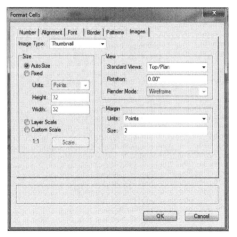

Image Sizing. Plenty to make your Worksheet look good as well as being very, very useful.

Left is a screengrab of the "Format Cells" Options.

12 WALLS, WINDOWS AND DOORS

In this chapter we will be looking at the Walls, Windows and Doors tools within the Building Shell Tool Set.

Before we start I must say that I haven't found these tools useful for theatrical scenic element construction drawings but for white card model visualisations and for creating your performance spaces they are invaluable. Just be aware what your final intended outcome is before reaching for these tools.

Lets start with the wall tool.

Clicking on the wall tool will bring up the familiar Left, Centre, Right and Custom control line options as discussed back in Chapter 1 with regard to the Double Line Tool.

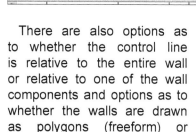

There are also options as to whether the control line is relative to the entire wall or relative to one of the wall components and options as to whether the walls are drawn as polygons (freeform) or rectangles.

The preferences button will bring up a window allowing you to specify the overall thickness of the wall and, if needed define components such as the thickness of timber and sheeting or perhaps brick, lath and plaster.

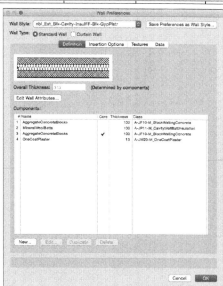

In the screengrab above we can see the component parts from one of the pre-set wall types. It comprises four components.

Concrete blocks, a layer of insulation, concrete blocks again then a one coat plaster finish.

Since this book is about using Vectorworks in a theatrical and entertainment environment I won't go any further into the building tools so we will revert back to the preferences window again and assume that we are either drawing up a simple performance space or drawing up a white card model for design purposes.

The wall style in my screengrab below has been left at "unstyled". I could rename this and save the preferences as a wall style for future use if desired using the button top right.

I have defined it as a notional 75mm Overall Thickness assuming it's a framed, on edge, built flat which will represent a wall with a window and door on stage.

Now, ensuring I have the correct control line selected I can simply begin to draw the wall flat and input the desired size in the floating toolbar. In this case I will make the flat 4880mm wide and will define a height of 7320mm in a moment.

I double click to finish the wall, since it's only a single flat.

If I select the wall and then look at the Object Info Palette I can see that the object is defined as a "Wall" and it has a number of parameters I can edit.

Firstly the height.

I can simply type 7320 in the height information box and leave everything else. Of course you should assign your flat to a class at this point to ensure good drawing management.

The only other button which is worth noting, as it may help you in the future if you decide to assign different colours or textures to the front and back of your model, is the "Reverse Sides" button.

Walls always have direction depending on the way they were drawn. I drew my wall left to right and therefore the "top" line in my plan view is the left side of the wall and the "bottom" line in plan view is the right side. If I'd drawn the wall right to left this would be reversed. It's important to know which is the left and right sides as colours and textures are assigned according to the right and left sides. However, if your wall ends up the wrong way or you have assigned colours or textures to the wrong sides you can use the "Reverse Sides" button to fix the error.

You can see the direction of a wall by selecting it with the Single Object Interactive Scaling Mode on.

The wall will show a blue arrow indicating the direction it was drawn.

I'm now ready to insert a door into the wall flat but will have a quick look from an isometric viewpoint and a quick OpenGL render just to make sure everything looks OK so far.

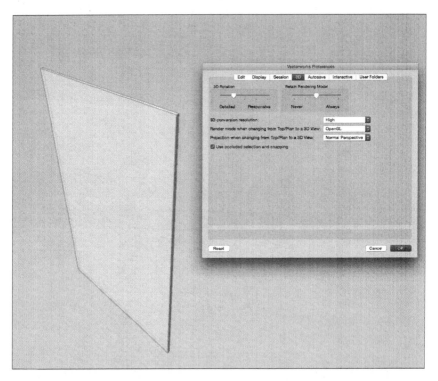

At this point Vectorworks has reset the Open GL Render and Normal Perspective. Therefore, I need to go back and change these back to my own preferences again of Wireframe and Orthogonal in the Vectorworks Preferences 3D Tab.

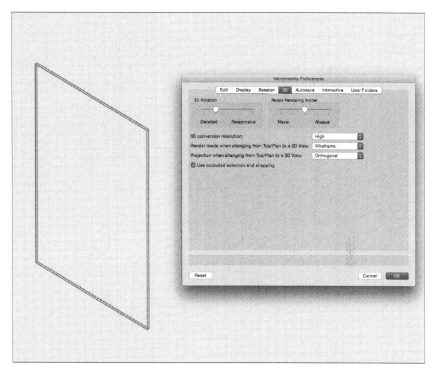

It's important to remember that you can only insert Doors and Windows into Walls. If I had drawn the wall as an extruded 4880 x 75 mm rectangle then tried to insert a door or window it wouldn't work. These high level, very editable, objects only work if inserted into "wall" defined objects.

It is possible to create walls using a different method using the Modify > Create Objects from Shapes command.

Firstly draw your 2D lines.

Ensure the 2D lines are selected then choose the Modify > Create Objects from Shapes command and you will be presented with an options window.

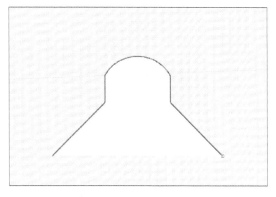

The Object Type "Walls" is at the bottom of the list.

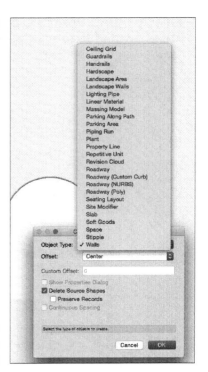

Select Walls as the Object Type then decide on the "offset" i.e. whether the 2D line is the left, right or centre of the wall you intend to create.

I have selected "Delete Source Shapes" as I don't need the original 2D line after the wall is created. Then click OK.

I now have six walls created from the original 2D line drawing and have full control of thickness, height, components, etc. from the Object Info Palette.

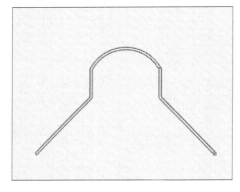

You may find this alternative method useful at some point but for now I will return to the simple stage flat to insert a door.

Make sure you are in Top/Plan view then choose the Door Tool.

After I choose the Door tool I have several options.

Firstly we have Standard or Offset Insertion Mode, which I will leave as "Standard". The Offset function is extremely useful if you knew, for example, that the edge of the door was a certain distance from a corner.

The option to Insert in Walls, which I will leave on and four Object Insertion modes, Left, Centre, Right and Object Origin, I will also leave as Object Origin. Again, if used in conjunction with the offset tool example above you would set this to be the edge of the door.

As I move my mouse, which should have the image of a door attached to it, over the wall, the wall will turn red. I can then click once to insert the door then, if I move my mouse around, I can define its orientation, then click again. Don't worry if you get this wrong as it is very easy to shuffle the door along the wall and change the orientation later.

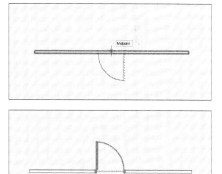

If you have the door selected then look at the Object Info Palette and you will see a huge number of editable properties.

I find it easier to double click the door and do any editing within the "Door Settings" Window.

Sometimes all you need to do is change the size of the door and decide whether to show it closed or ajar on your plans and

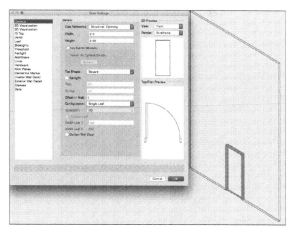

renders but there are a huge number of other editable options giving you the option to create simple structural openings to complex arrangements.

Further clarification for each of the editable properties can be found in the excellent Vectorworks help menu so I won't take up the remainder of the book duplicating that information here.

It's worth pointing out a couple of notes, which aren't so obvious.

The doors have Interior and Exterior Wall Detail parameters. These are defined by the wall as mentioned previously. The orientation of the door, whether inward or outward, and any flipping, wont change the definition of interior or exterior which is defined by the wall. The exterior is always the left hand side of the wall.

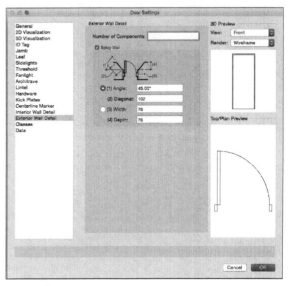

For example, the two screengrabs to the right I have drawn the top wall first left to right, (exterior top line) then the bottom wall right to left (exterior bottom line). The doors have been inserted the same way and an Exterior Splay of 45 degrees given to the Door.

You can see that the splay is different in each of the pictures because of the orientation, i.e. the exterior of the wall, not the door.

Furthermore, you

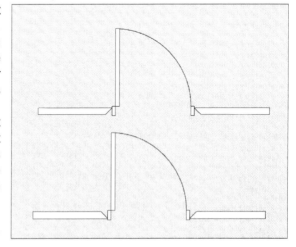

should be aware that bringing in these high level complex objects such as doors and windows will, by default, bring in new classes. Even my very simple drawing has new classes of Glazing and Sills and associated Renderworks Texture for the Glass.

Classes for the different parts of the door can either be controlled by the overall Door Class or be attributed individually using the Classes menu of the Door Settings window. Here you can see that the Class for Glazing, Sidelights and Fanlights has already been set as "Glazing-Clear" and that Renderworks Texture has been imported into the drawing even if it is used or not.

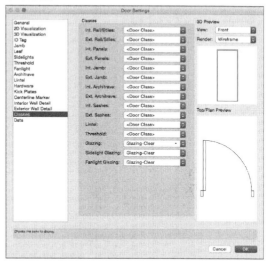

I'm going to go back to the General Tab and change the Doors in my flat to be Large Double Doors with a Round Top.

I'm also going to open the 3D Visualisation Tab and select.

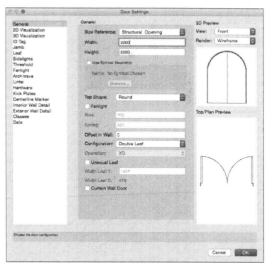

Draw 3D Open and Type 45 into the Open Angle.

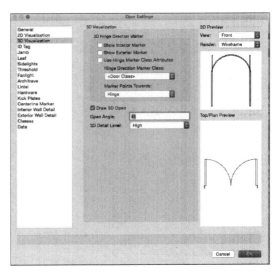

If I look at my Flat in 3D now I can see my Double Doors clearly.

I'm now going to place a window above the door.

I tend to always return to Top/Plan View before inserting Doors and Windows. It's not absolutely necessary but I find it much easier to place items accurately in top / plan view.

Choose the Window Tool then, as with the door tool, place your mouse over the wall and it will glow red. Click once to insert and again to set the orientation. The window orientation may not be as obvious as when inserting the door but again, don't worry, it can be edited later by "Flipping" in the

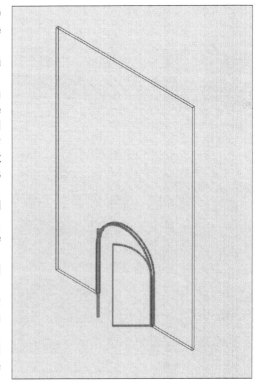

Object Info Palette.

As with the Door Tool the Window Tool has a huge number of editable characteristics, which can all be explored

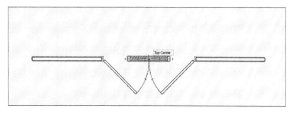

using the Vectorworks help menu and experimenting.

In this example I have chosen to make the window a large circle the same width as the door and set the height using the sill of the window as the reference point (the alternative is the head of the window).

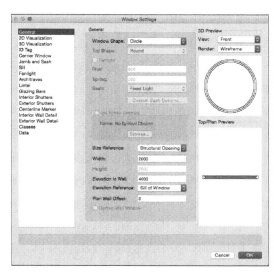
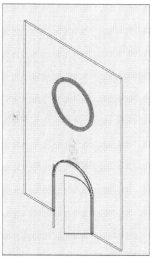

Since this is only a white card model I can simply produce a nice render by creating a Viewport and sending it to a new Sheet Layer.

Within the Viewport I can create a Foreground and Background Render.

With the Viewport selected I have chosen a Background Render > Renderworks Style > Realistic Colours White and a Foreground Render of Hidden Line.

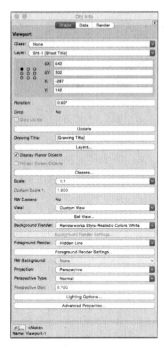

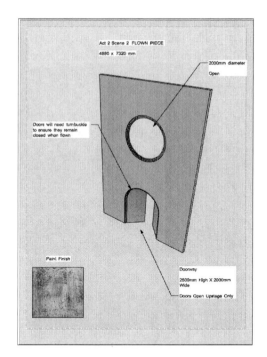

Act 2 Scene 2 FLOWN PIECE

4880 x 7320 mm

2000mm diameter
Open

Doors will need turnbuckle
to ensure they remain
closed when flown

Paint Finish

Doorway

2500mm High X 2000mm
Wide

Doors Open Upstage Only

All this needs now is the addition of a few annotations showing sizes and intended finishes for the concept or white card model meeting.

The Wall, Doors and Windows are obviously all very useful for creating a 3D representation of your venue or performance space.

I normally just use the generic "Unstyled" wall setting again but with a 150mm thickness.

In this example the wall tool has been used to create the walls of the stage area and the proscenium area.

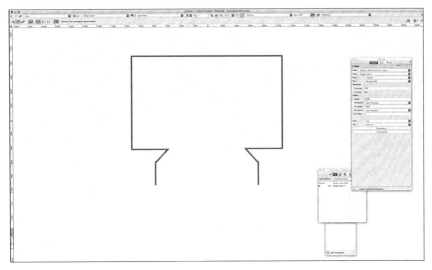

The Door Tool can be added to create the large dock doors on either side of the stage and the normal sized pass doors, downstage in either wing.

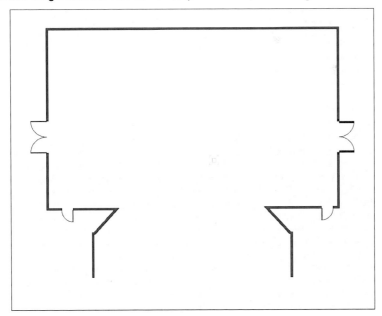

This quick representation of the stage was created in around ten minutes and could form the basis of a much more complex model or just be used to visualise design concepts in early development.

To create the Proscenium Opening I can just create another wall and inset a "Door" which will be a structural opening of 11200mm x 7200mm.

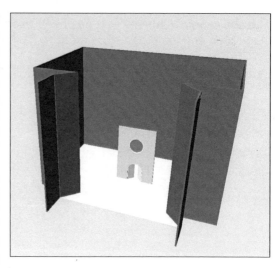

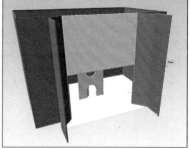

In Vectorworks 2015 it became possible to create complex wall shapes by using the new rectangle mode for drawing walls. Walls will automatically join with adjacent walls and holding the Alt key will remove sections already drawn.

This first screengrab was created by drawing a large rectangle then a smaller "room" rectangle. The internal and external walls automatically joined.

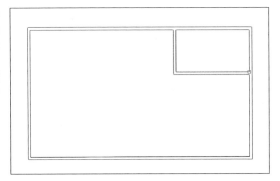

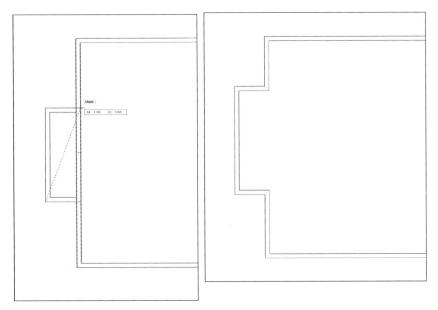

This Alcove was created by Drawing a second Rectangle over the existing left hand wall while holding down the Alt key.

As a final tip, the Trim Tool in the Basic Tool Palette can remove sections of walls between two joins.

A combination of the standard Polygon tool and the New Rectangle Tool should allow you to create walls, for whatever purpose, quickly and easily.

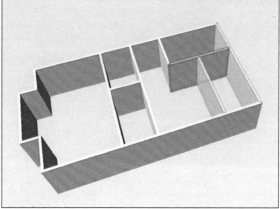

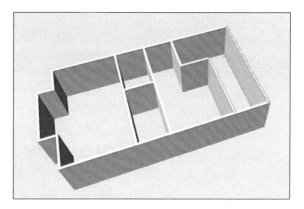

ENTERTAINMENT TECHNOLOGY PRESS

FREE SUBSCRIPTION SERVICE

Keeping Up To Date with

Vectorworks for Theatre

Entertainment Technology titles are continually up-dated, and all major changes and additions are listed in date order in the relevant dedicated area of the publisher's website. Simply go to the front page of www.etnow.com and click on the BOOKS button. From there you can locate the title and be connected through to the latest information and services related to the publication.

The author of the title welcomes comments and suggestions about the book and can be contacted by email at:
S.Macluskie@rcs.ac.uk

Titles Published by Entertainment Technology Press

50 Rigging Calls *Chris Higgs, Cristiano Giavedoni 246pp* **£16.95**
ISBN: 9781904031758
Chris Higgs, author of ETP's two leading titles on rigging, An Introduction to Rigging in the Entertainment Industry and Rigging for Entertainment: Regulations and Practice, has collected together 50 articles he has provided regularly for Lighting + Sound International magazine from 2005 to date. They provide a wealth of information for those practising the craft within the entertainment technology industry. The book is profusely illustrated with caricature drawings by Christiano Giavedoni, featuring the popular rigging expert Mario.

ABC of Theatre Jargon *Francis Reid 106pp* **£9.95** ISBN: 9781904031093
This glossary of theatrical terminology explains the common words and phrases that are used in normal conversation between actors, directors, designers, technicians and managers.

Aluminium Structures in the Entertainment Industry *Peter Hind 234pp* **£24.95**
ISBN: 9781904031062
Aluminium Structures in the Entertainment Industry aims to educate the reader in all aspects of the design and safe usage of temporary and permanent aluminium structures specific to the entertainment industry – such as roof structures, PA towers, temporary staging, etc.

AutoCAD – A Handbook for Theatre Users *David Ripley 340pp* **£29.95**
ISBN: 9781904031741
From 'Setting Up' to 'Drawing in Three Dimensions' via 'Drawings Within Drawings', this compact and fully illustrated guide to AutoCAD covers everything from the basics to full colour rendering and remote 3D plotting. Third, completely revised edition, June 2014.

Automation in the Entertainment Industry – A User's Guide *Mark Ager and John Hastie 382pp* **£29.95** ISBN: 9781904031581
In the last 15 years, there has been a massive growth in the use of automation in entertainment, especially in theatres, and it is now recognised as its own discipline. However, it is still only used in around 5% of theatres worldwide. In the next 25 years, given current growth patterns, that figure will rise to 30%. This will mean that the majority of theatre personnel, including directors, designers, technical staff, actors and theatre management, will come into contact with automation for the first time at some point in their careers. This book is intended to provide insights and practical advice from those who use automation, to help the first-time user understand the issues and avoid the pitfalls in its implementation.

Basics – A Beginner's Guide to Lighting Design *Peter Coleman 92pp* **£9.95**
ISBN: 9781904031413
The fourth in the author's 'Basics' series, this title covers the subject area in four main sections: The Concept, Practical Matters, Related Issues and The Design Into Practice. In an

area that is difficult to be definitive, there are several things that cross all the boundaries of all lighting design and it's these areas that the author seeks to help with.

Basics – A Beginner's Guide to Special Effects *Peter Coleman 82pp* **£9.95**
ISBN: 9781904031338
This title introduces newcomers to the world of special effects. It describes all types of special effects including pyrotechnic, smoke and lighting effects, projections, noise machines, etc. It places emphasis on the safe storage, handling and use of pyrotechnics.

Basics – A Beginner's Guide to Stage Lighting *Peter Coleman 86pp* **£9.95**
ISBN: 9781904031208
This title does what it says: it introduces newcomers to the world of stage lighting. It will not teach the reader the art of lighting design, but will teach beginners much about the 'nuts and bolts' of stage lighting.

Basics – A Beginner's Guide to Stage Sound *Peter Coleman 86pp* **£9.95**
ISBN: 9781904031277
This title does what it says: it introduces newcomers to the world of stage sound. It will not teach the reader the art of sound design, but will teach beginners much about the background to sound reproduction in a theatrical environment.

Basics: A Beginner's Guide to Stage Management *Peter Coleman 64pp* **£7.95**
ISBN: 9781904031475
The fifth in Peter Coleman's popular 'Basics' series, this title provides a practical insight into, and the definition of, the role of stage management. Further chapters describe Cueing or 'Calling' the Show (the Prompt Book), and the Hardware and Training for Stage Management. This is a book about people and systems, without which most of the technical equipment used by others in the performance workplace couldn't function.

Building Better Theaters *Michael Mell 180pp* **£16.95** ISBN: 9781904031406
A title within our Consultancy Series, this book describes the process of designing a theatre, from the initial decision to build through to opening night. Michael Mell's book provides a step-by-step guide to the design and construction of performing arts facilities. Chapters discuss: assembling your team, selecting an architect, different construction methods, the architectural design process, construction of the theatre, theatrical systems and equipment, the stage, backstage, the auditorium, ADA requirements and the lobby. Each chapter clearly describes what to expect and how to avoid surprises. It is a must-read for architects, planners, performing arts groups, educators and anyone who may be considering building or renovating a theatre.

Carry on Fading *Francis Reid 216pp* **£20.00** ISBN: 9781904031642
This is a record of five of the best years of the author's life. Years so good that the only downside is the pangs of guilt at enjoying such contentment in a world full of misery induced by greed, envy and imposed ideologies. Fortunately Francis' DNA is high on luck, optimism and blessing counting.

Case Studies in Crowd Management

Chris Kemp, Iain Hill, Mick Upton, Mark Hamilton 206pp **£16.95**
ISBN: 9781904031482
This important work has been compiled from a series of research projects carried out by the staff of the Centre for Crowd Management and Security Studies at Buckinghamshire Chilterns University College (now Bucks New University), and seminar work carried out in Berlin and Groningen with partner Yourope. It includes case studies, reports and a crowd management safety plan for a major outdoor rock concert, safe management of rock concerts utilising a triple barrier safety system and pan-European Health & Safety Issues.

Case Studies in Crowd Management, Security and Business Continuity

Chris Kemp, Patrick Smith 274pp **£24.95** ISBN: 9781904031635
The creation of good case studies to support work in progress and to give answers to those seeking guidance in their quest to come to terms with perennial questions is no easy task. The first Case Studies in Crowd Management book focused mainly on a series of festivals and events that had a number of issues which required solving. This book focuses on a series of events that had major issues that impacted on the every day delivery of the events researched.

Close Protection – The Softer Skills *Geoffrey Padgham 132pp* **£11.95**
ISBN: 9781904031390
This is the first educational book in a new 'Security Series' for Entertainment Technology Press, and it coincides with the launch of the new 'Protective Security Management' Foundation Degree at Buckinghamshire Chilterns University College (now Bucks New University). The author is a former full-career Metropolitan Police Inspector from New Scotland Yard with 27 years' experience of close protection (CP). For 22 of those years he specialised in operations and senior management duties with the Royalty Protection Department at Buckingham Palace, followed by five years in the private security industry specialising in CP training design and delivery. His wealth of protection experience comes across throughout the text, which incorporates sound advice and exceptional practical guidance, subtly separating fact from fiction. This publication is an excellent form of reference material for experienced operatives, students and trainees.

A Comparative Study of Crowd Behaviour at Two Major Music Events

Chris Kemp, Iain Hill, Mick Upton 78pp **£7.95** ISBN: 9781904031253
A compilation of the findings of reports made at two major live music concerts, and in particular crowd behaviour, which is followed from ingress to egress.

Control Freak *Wayne Howell 270pp* **£28.95** ISBN: 9781904031550
Control Freak is the second book by Wayne Howell. It provides an in depth study of DMX512 and the new RDM (Remote Device Management) standards. The book is aimed at both users and developers and provides a wealth of real world information based on the author's twenty year experience of lighting control.

Copenhagen Opera House   *Richard Brett and John Offord 272pp*   **£32.00**
ISBN: 9781904031420
Completed in a little over three years, the Copenhagen Opera House opened with a royal gala performance on 15th January 2005. Built on a spacious brown-field site, the building is a landmark venue and this book provides the complete technical background story to an opera house set to become a benchmark for future design and planning. Sixteen chapters by relevant experts involved with the project cover everything from the planning of the auditorium and studio stage, the stage engineering, stage lighting and control and architectural lighting through to acoustic design and sound technology plus technical summaries.

Cue 80   *Francis Reid 310pp*   **£17.95**   ISBN: 9781904031659
Although Francis Reid's work in theatre has been visual rather than verbal, writing has provided crucial support. Putting words on paper has been the way in which he organised and clarified his thoughts. And in his self-confessed absence of drawing skills, writing has helped him find words to communicate his visual thinking in discussions with the rest of the creative team. As a by-product, this process of searching for the right words to help formulate and analyse ideas has resulted in half-a-century of articles in theatre journals.
Cue 80 is an anthology of these articles and is released in celebration of Francis' 80th birthday.

The DMX 512-A Handbook – Design and Implementation of DMX Enabled Products and Networks   *James Eade 150pp*   **£13.95**   ISBN: 9781904031727
This guidebook was originally conceived as a guide to the new DMX512-A standard on behalf of the ESTA Controls Protocols Working Group (CPWG). It has subsequently been updated and is aimed at all levels of reader from technicians working with or servicing equipment in the field as well as manufacturers looking to build in DMX control to their lighting products. It also gives thorough guidance to consultants and designers looking to design DMX networks.

Electric Shadows: an Introduction to Video and Projection on Stage   *Nick Moran 234pp*
£23.95   ISBN: 9781904031734
Electric Shadows aims to guide the emerging video designer through the many simple and difficult technical and aesthetic choices and decisions he or she has to make in taking their design from outline idea through to realisation. The main body of the book takes the reader through the process of deciding what content will be projected onto what screen or screens to make the best overall production design. The book will help you make electric shadows that capture the attention of your audience, to help you tell your stories in just the way you want.

Electrical Safety for Live Events   *Marco van Beek 98pp*   **£16.95**   ISBN: 9781904031284
This title covers electrical safety regulations and good practise pertinent to the entertainment industries and includes some basic electrical theory as well as clarifying the "do's and don't's" of working with electricity.

Entertainment Electronics   *Anton Woodward 154pp*   **£15.95**   ISBN: 9781904031819
Electronic engineering in theatres has become quite prevalent in recent years, whether for lighting, sound, automation or props – so it has become an increasingly important skill for

the theatre technician to possess. This book is intended to give the theatre technician a good grasp of the fundamental principles of electronics without getting too bogged down with maths so that many of the mysteries of electronics are revealed.

Entertainment in Production Volume 1: 1994-1999 *Rob Halliday 254pp* **£24.95**
ISBN: 9781904031512

Entertainment in Production Volume 2: 2000-2006 *Rob Halliday 242poo* £24.95
ISBN: 9781904031529
Rob Halliday has a dual career as a lighting designer/programmer and author and in these two volumes he provides the intriguing but comprehensive technical background stories behind the major musical productions and other notable projects spanning the period 1994 to 2005. Having been closely involved with the majority of the events described, the author is able to present a first-hand and all-encompassing portrayal of how many of the major shows across the past decade came into being. From *Oliver!* and *Miss Saigon* to *Mamma Mia!* and *Mary Poppins*, here the complete technical story unfolds. The books, which are profusely illustrated, are in large part an adapted selection of articles that first appeared in the magazine *Lighting&Sound International*.

Entertainment Technology Yearbook 2008 *John Offord 220pp* **£14.95**
ISBN: 9781904031543
The Entertainment Technology Yearbook 2008 covers the year 2007 and includes picture coverage of major industry exhibitions in Europe compiled from the pages of Entertainment Technology magazine and the etnow.com website, plus articles and pictures of production, equipment and project highlights of the year.

The Exeter Theatre Fire *David Anderson 202pp* **£24.95** ISBN: 9781904031130
This title is a fascinating insight into the events that led up to the disaster at the Theatre Royal, Exeter, on the night of September 5th 1887. The book details what went wrong, and the lessons that were learned from the event.

Fading into Retirement *Francis Reid 124pp* **£17.95**
ISBN: 9781904031352
This is the final book in Francis Reid's fading trilogy which, with Fading Light and Carry on Fading, updates the Hearing the Light record of places visited, performances seen, and people met. Never say never, but the author uses the 'final' label because decreasing mobility means that his ability to travel is diminished to the point that his life is now contained within a very few square miles. His memories are triggered by over 600 CDs, half of them Handel and 100 or so DVDs supplemented by a rental subscription to LOVEFiLM.

Fading Light – A Year in Retirement *Francis Reid 136pp* **£14.95**
ISBN: 9781904031352
Francis Reid, the lighting industry's favourite author, describes a full year in retirement. "Old age is much more fun than I expected," he says. Fading Light describes visits and experiences to the author's favourite theatres and opera houses, places of relaxation and re-visits to scholarly institutions.

Focus on Lighting Technology *Richard Cadena 120pp* **£17.95** ISBN: 9781904031147
This concise work unravels the mechanics behind modern performance lighting and appeals to designers and technicians alike. Packed with clear, easy-to-read diagrams, the book provides excellent explanations behind the technology of performance lighting.

The Followspot Guide *Nick Mobsby 450pp* **£28.95** ISBN: 9781904031499
The first in ETP's Equipment Series, Nick Mobsby's Followspot Guide tells you everything you need to know about followspots, from their history through to maintenance and usage. Its pages include a technical specification of 193 followspots from historical to the latest versions from major manufacturers.

From Ancient Rome to Rock 'n' Roll – a Review of the UK Leisure Security Industry *Mick Upton 198pp* **£14.95** ISBN: 9781904031505
From stewarding, close protection and crowd management through to his engagement as a senior consultant Mick Upton has been ever present in the events industry. A founder of ShowSec International in 1982 he was its chairman until 2000. The author has led the way on training within the sector. He set up the ShowSec Training Centre and has acted as a consultant at the Bramshill Police College. He has been prominent in the development of courses at Buckinghamshire New University where he was awarded a Doctorate in 2005. Mick has received numerous industry awards. His book is a personal account of the development and professionalism of the sector across the past 50 years.

Gobos for Image Projection *Michael Hall and Julie Harper 176pp* **£25.95**
ISBN: 9781904031628
In this first published book dedicated totally to the gobo, the authors take the reader through from the history of projection to the development of the present day gobo. And there is broad practical advice and ample reference information to back it up. A feature of the work is the inclusion, interspersed throughout the text, of comment and personal experience in the use and application of gobos from over 25 leading lighting designers worldwide.

Health and Safety Aspects in the Live Music Industry *Chris Kemp, Iain Hill 300pp* **£30.00** ISBN: 9781904031222
This major work includes chapters on various safety aspects of live event production and is written by specialists in their particular areas of expertise.

Health and Safety in the Live Music and Event Technical Produciton Industry *Chris Hannam 74pp* **£12.95** ISBN: 9781904031802
This book covers the real basics of health and safety in the live music and event production industry in a simple jargon free manner that can also be used as the perfect student course note accompaniment to the various safety passport schemes that now exist in our industry.

Health and Safety Management in the Live Music and Events Industry *Chris Hannam 480pp* **£25.95** ISBN: 9781904031307
This title covers the health and safety regulations and their application regarding all aspects

of staging live entertainment events, and is an invaluable manual for production managers and event organisers.

Hearing the Light – 50 Years Backstage *Francis Reid 280pp* **£24.95**
ISBN: 9781904031185
This highly enjoyable memoir delves deeply into the theatricality of the industry. The author's almost fanatical interest in opera, his formative period as lighting designer at Glyndebourne and his experiences as a theatre administrator, writer and teacher make for a broad and unique background.

Introduction to Live Sound *Roland Higham 174pp* **£16.95**
ISBN: 9781904031796
This new title aims to provide working engineers and newcomers alike with a concise knowledge base that explains some of the theory and principles that they will encounter every day. It should provide for the student and newcomer to the field a valuable compendium of helpful knowledge.

An Introduction to Rigging in the Entertainment Industry *Chris Higgs 272pp* **£24.95**
ISBN: 9781904031123
This title is a practical guide to rigging techniques and practices and also thoroughly covers safety issues and discusses the implications of working within recommended guidelines and regulations. Second edition revised September 2008.

Let There be Light – Entertainment Lighting Software Pioneers in Conversation
Robert Bell 390pp **£32.00** ISBN: 9781904031246
Robert Bell interviews a distinguished group of software engineers working on entertainment lighting ideas and products.

Light and Colour Filters *Michael Hall and Eddie Ruffell 286pp* **£23.95**
ISBN: 9781904031598
Written by two acknowledged and respected experts in the field, this book is destined to become the standard reference work on the subject. The title chronicles the development and use of colour filters and also describes how colour is perceived and how filters function. Up-to-date reference tables will help the practitioner make better and more specific choices of colour.

Lighting for Roméo and Juliette *John Offord 172pp* **£26.95** ISBN: 9781904031161
John Offord describes the making of the Vienna State Opera production from the lighting designer's viewpoint – from the point where director Jürgen Flimm made his decision not to use scenery or sets and simply employ the expertise of lighting designer Patrick Woodroffe.

Lighting Systems for TV Studios *Nick Mobsby 570pp* **£45.00** ISBN: 9781904031000
Lighting Systems for TV Studios, now in its second edition, is the first book specifically written on the subject and has become the 'standard' resource work for studio planning and design covering the key elements of system design, luminaires, dimming, control,

data networks and suspension systems as well as detailing the infrastructure items such as cyclorama, electrical and ventilation. TV lighting principles are explained and some history on TV broadcasting, camera technology and the equipment is provided to help set the scene! The second edition includes applications for sine wave and distributed dimming, moving lights, Ethernet and new cool lamp technology.

Lighting Techniques for Theatre-in-the-Round *Jackie Staines 188pp* **£24.95**
ISBN: 9781904031017
Lighting Techniques for Theatre-in-the-Round is a unique reference source for those working on lighting design for theatre-in-the-round for the first time. It is the first title to be published specifically on the subject and it also provides some anecdotes and ideas for more challenging shows, and attempts to blow away some of the myths surrounding lighting in this format.

Lighting the Diamond Jubilee Concert *Durham Marenghi 102pp* **£19.95**
ISBN: 9781904031673
In this highly personal landmark document the show's lighting designer Durham Marenghi pays tribute to the team of industry experts who each played an important role in bringing the Diamond Jubilee Concert to fruition, both for television and live audiences. The book contains colour production photography throughout and describes the production processes and the thinking behind them. In his Foreword, BBC Executive Producer Guy Freeman states: "Working with the whole lighting team on such a special project was a real treat for me and a fantastic achievement for them, which the pages of this book give a remarkable insight into."

Lighting the Stage *Francis Reid 120pp* **£14.95** ISBN: 9781904031086
Lighting the Stage discusses the human relationships involved in lighting design – both between people, and between these people and technology. The book is written from a highly personal viewpoint and its 'thinking aloud' approach is one that Francis Reid has used in his writings over the past 30 years.

Miscellany of Lighting and Stagecraft *Michael Hall & Julie Harper 222pp* **£22.95**
ISBN: 9781904031680
This title will help schools, colleges, amateurs, technicians and all those interested in practical theatre and performance to understand, in an entertaining and informative way, the key backstage skills. Within its pages, numerous professionals share their own special knowledge and expertise, interspersed with diversions of historic interest and anecdotes from those practising at the front line of the industry. As a result, much of the advice and skills set out have not previously been set in print. The editors' intention with this book is to provide a Miscellany that is not ordered or categorised in strict fashion, but rather encourages the reader to flick through or dip into it, finding nuggets of information and anecdotes to entertain, inspire and engender curiosity – also to invite further research or exploration and generally encourage people to enter the industry and find out for themselves.

Mr Phipps' Theatre *Mark Jones, John Pick 172pp* £17.95 ISBN: 9781904031383
Mark Jones and John Pick describe "The Sensational Story of Eastbourne's Royal
Hippodrome" – formerly Eastbourne Theatre Royal. An intriguing narrative, the book sets
the story against a unique social history of the town. Peter Longman, former director of The
Theatres Trust, provides the Foreword.

Northen Lights *Michael Northen 256pp* **£17.95** ISBN: 9781904031666
Many books have been written by famous personalities in the theatre about their lives and
work. However this is probably one of the first memoirs by someone who has spent his
entire career behind scenes, and not in front of the footlights. As a lighting designer and as
consultant to designers and directors, Michael Northen worked through an exciting period
of fifty years of theatrical history from the late nineteen thirties in theatres in the UK and
abroad, and on productions ranging from Shakespeare, opera and ballet to straight plays,
pantomimes and cabaret. This is not a complicated technical text book, but is intended to
give an insight into some of the 300 productions in which he had been involved and some
of the directors, the designers and backstage staff he have worked with, viewed from a new
angle.

Pages From Stages *Anthony Field 204pp* **£17.95** ISBN: 9781904031260
Anthony Field explores the changing style of theatres including interior design, exterior
design, ticket and seat prices, and levels of service, while questioning whether the theatre
still exists as a place of entertainment for regular theatre-goers.

People, Places, Performances *Remembered by Francis Reid 60pp* **£8.95**
ISBN: 9781904031765
In growing older, the Author has found that memories, rather than featuring the events,
increasingly tend to focus on the people who caused them, the places where they happened
and the performances that arose. So Francis Reid has used these categories in endeavouring to
compile a brief history of the second half of the twentieth century.

Performing Arts Technical Training Handbook 2013/2014 *ed: John Offord 304pp*
£19.95 ISBN: 9781904031710
Published in association with the ABTT (Association of British Theatre Technicians), this
important Handbook, now in its third edition, includes fully detailed and indexed entries
describing courses on backstage crafts offered by over 100 universities and colleges across
the UK. A completely new research project, with accompanying website, the title also
includes articles with advice for those considering a career 'behind the scenes', together
with contact information and descriptions of the major organisations involved with industry
training – plus details of companies offering training within their own premises.

Practical Dimming *Nick Mobsby 364pp* **£22.95** ISBN: 97819040313444
This important and easy to read title covers the history of electrical and electronic dimming,
how dimmers work, current dimmer types from around the world, planning of a dimming
system, looking at new sine wave dimming technology and distributed dimming. Integration
of dimming into different performance venues as well as the necessary supporting electrical

systems are fully detailed. Significant levels of information are provided on the many different forms and costs of potential solutions as well as how to plan specific solutions. Architectural dimming for the likes of hotels, museums and shopping centres is included. Practical Dimming is a companion book to Practical DMX and is designed for all involved in the use, operation and design of dimming systems.

Practical DMX *Nick Mobsby 276pp* **£16.95** ISBN: 9781904031369
In this highly topical and important title the author details the principles of DMX, how to plan a network, how to choose equipment and cables, with data on products from around the world, and how to install DMX networks for shows and on a permanently installed basis. The easy style of the book and the helpful fault finding tips, together with a review of different DMX testing devices provide an ideal companion for all lighting technicians and system designers. An introduction to Ethernet and Canbus networks are provided as well as tips on analogue networks and protocol conversion. It also includes a chapter on Remote Device Management.

A Practical Guide to Health and Safety in the Entertainment Industry
Marco van Beek 120pp **£14.95** ISBN: 9781904031048
This book is designed to provide a practical approach to Health and Safety within the Live Entertainment and Event industry. It gives industry-pertinent examples, and seeks to break down the myths surrounding Health and Safety.

Production Management *Joe Aveline 134pp* **£17.95** ISBN: 9781904031109
Joe Aveline's book is an in-depth guide to the role of the Production Manager, and includes real-life practical examples and 'Aveline's Fables' – anecdotes of his experiences with real messages behind them.

Rigging for Entertainment: Regulations and Practice *Chris Higgs 156pp* **£19.95**
ISBN: 9781904031215
Continuing where he left off with his highly successful An Introduction to Rigging in the Entertainment Industry, Chris Higgs' second title covers the regulations and use of equipment in greater detail.

Rock Solid Ethernet *Wayne Howell 304pp* **£23.95** ISBN: 9781904031697
Now in its third completely revised and reset edition, Rock Solid Ethernet is aimed specifically at specifiers, installers and users of entertainment industry systems, and will give the reader a thorough grounding in all aspects of computer networks, whatever industry they may work in. The inclusion of historical and technical 'sidebars' make for an enjoyable as well as an informative read.

Sixty Years of Light Work *Fred Bentham 450pp* **£26.95** ISBN: 9781904031079
This title is an autobiography of one of the great names behind the development of modern stage lighting equipment and techniques. It includes a complete facsimile of the famous Strand Electric Catalogue of May 1936 – a reference work in itself.

Sound for the Stage *Patrick Finelli 218pp* **£24.95** ISBN: 9781904031154
Patrick Finelli's thorough manual covering all aspects of live and recorded sound for performance is a complete training course for anyone interested in working in the field of stage sound, and is a must for any student of sound.

Stage Automation *Anton Woodward 128pp* **£12.95** ISBN: 9781904031567
The purpose of this book is to explain the stage automation techniques used in modern theatre to achieve some of the spectacular visual effects seen in recent years. The book is targeted at automation operators, production managers, theatre technicians, stage engineering machinery manufacturers and theatre engineering students. Topics are covered in sufficient detail to provide an insight into the thought processes that the stage automation engineer has to consider when designing a control system to control stage machinery in a modern theatre. The author has worked on many stage automation projects and developed the award-winning Impressario stage automation system.

Stage Lighting Design in Britain: The Emergence of the Lighting Designer, 1881-1950
Nigel Morgan 300pp **£17.95** ISBN: 9781904031345
This title sets out to ascertain the main course of events and the controlling factors that determined the emergence of the theatre lighting designer in Britain, starting with the introduction of incandescent electric light to the stage, and ending at the time of the first public lighting design credits around 1950. The book explores the practitioners, equipment, installations and techniques of lighting design.

Stage Lighting for Theatre Designers *Nigel Morgan 124pp* **£17.95**
ISBN: 9781904031192
This is an updated second edition of Nigel Morgan's popular book for students of theatre design – outlining all the techniques of stage lighting design.

Technical Marketing Techniques *David Brooks, Andy Collier, Steve Norman 160pp*
£24.95 ISBN: 9781904031031
Technical Marketing is a novel concept, defined and elaborated by the authors of this book, with business-to-business companies competing in fast developing technical product sectors.

Technical Standards for Places of Entertainment *ABTT 354pp A4* **£45.00**
ISBN: 9781904031703
Technical Standards for Places of Entertainment details the necessary physical standards required for entertainment venues. Known in the industry as the "Yellow Book" the latest completely revised edition was first published in June 2013.

Theatre Engineering and Stage Machinery *Toshiro Ogawa 332pp* **£30.00**
ISBN: 9781904031024
Theatre Engineering and Stage Machinery is a unique reference work covering every aspect of theatrical machinery and stage technology in global terms, and across the complete historical spectrum. Revised February 2007.

Theatre Lighting in the Age of Gas *Terence Rees 232pp* **£24.95**
ISBN: 9781904031178
Entertainment Technology Press has republished this valuable historic work previously produced by the Society for Theatre Research in 1978. Theatre Lighting in the Age of Gas investigates the technological and artistic achievements of theatre lighting engineers from the 1700s to the late Victorian period.

Theatre Space: A Rediscovery Reported *Francis Reid 238pp* **£19.95**
ISBN: 9781904031437
In the post-war world of the 1950s and 60s, the format of theatre space became a matter for a debate that aroused passions of an intensity unknown before or since. The proscenium arch was clearly identified as the enemy, accused of forming a barrier to disrupt the relations between the actor and audience. An uneasy fellow-traveller at the time, Francis Reid later recorded his impressions whilst enjoying performances or working in theatres old and new and this book is an important collection of his writings in various theatrical journals from 1969-2001 including his contribution to the Cambridge Guide to the Theatre in 1988. It reports some of the flavour of the period when theatre architecture was rediscovering its past in a search to establish its future.

The Theatres and Concert Halls of Fellner and Helmer *Michael Sell 246pp* **£23.95**
ISBN: 9781904031772
This is the first British study of the works of the prolific Fellner and Helmer Atelier which was active from 1871-1914 during which time they produced over 80 theatre designs and are second in quantity only to Frank Matcham, to whom reference is made.
This period is one of great change as a number of serious theatre fires which included Nice and Vienna had the effect of the introduction of safety legislation which affected theatre design. This study seeks to show how Fellner and Helmer and Frank Matcham dealt with this increasing safety legislation, in particular the way in which safety was built into their new three part theatres equipped with iron stages, safety curtains, electricity and appropriate access and egress and, in the Vienna practice, how this was achieved across 13 countries.

Theatres of Achievement *John Higgins 302pp* **£29.95** ISBN: 9781904031376
John Higgins affectionately describes the history of 40 distinguished UK theatres in a personal tribute, each uniquely illustrated by the author. Completing each profile is colour photography by Adrian Eggleston.

Theatric Tourist *Francis Reid 220pp* **£19.95** ISBN: 9781904031468
Theatric Tourist is the delightful story of Francis Reid's visits across more than 50 years to theatres, theatre museums, performances and even movie theme parks. In his inimitable style, the author involves the reader within a personal experience of venues from the Legacy of Rome to theatres of the Renaissance and Eighteenth Century Baroque and the Gustavian Theatres of Stockholm. His performance experiences include Wagner in Beyreuth, the Pleasures of Tivoli and Wayang in Singapore. This is a 'must have' title for those who are as "incurably stagestruck" as the author.

Through the Viewfinder *Jeremy Hoare 276pp* **£21.95** ISBN:: 9781904031574
Do you want to be a top television cameraman? Well this is going to help!
Through the Viewfinder is aimed at media students wanting to be top professional television
cameramen – but it will also be of interest to anyone who wants to know what goes on
behind the cameras that bring so much into our homes.
The author takes his own opinionated look at how to operate a television camera based on
23 years' experience looking through many viewfinders for a major ITV network company.
Based on interviews with people he has worked with, all leaders in the profession, the book
is based on their views and opinions and is a highly revealing portrait of what happens
behind the scenes in television production from a cameraman's point of view.

Vectorworks for Theatre *Steve Macluskie 232pp* **£23.95** ISBN: 9781904031826
An essential reference manual for anyone using Vectorworks in the Theatre Industry. This
book covers everything from introducing the basic tools to creating 3D design concepts and
using worksheets to calculate stock usage and lighting design paperwork. A highly visual
style using hundreds of high resolution screen images makes this a very easy book to follow
whether novice or experienced user.

Walt Disney Concert Hall – The Backstage Story *Patricia MacKay & Richard Pilbrow*
250pp **£28.95** ISBN: 9781904031239
Spanning the 16-year history of the design and construction of the Walt Disney Concert
Hall, this book provides a fresh and detailed behind the scenes story of the design and
technology from a variety of viewpoints. This is the first book to reveal the "process" of the
design of a concert hall.

Yesterday's Lights – A Revolution Reported *Francis Reid 352pp* **£26.95**
ISBN: 9781904031321
Set to help new generations to be aware of where the art and science of theatre lighting is
coming from – and stimulate a nostalgia trip for those who lived through the period, Francis
Reid's latest book has over 350 pages dedicated to the task, covering the 'revolution' from
the fifties through to the present day. Although this is a highly personal account of the
development of lighting design and technology and he admits that there are 'gaps', you'd be
hard put to find anything of significance missing.

Go to www.etbooks.co.uk for full details of above titles and secure online ordering facilities.
Most books also available for Kindle.